Fifty Days for a Firm Foundation

A Fifty-Day Devotional for a Foundation Built on Solid Biblical Principles

Rick Joyner

202-41

MorningStar Publications

A DIVISION OF MORNINGSTAR FELLOWSHIP CHURCH
P.O. Box 440
Wilkesboro, NC 28697

Table of Contents

Introduction 5

Day 1—The Beginning 9

Day 2—The Plan 11

Day 3—The Spirit Moves 13

Day 4—The Light 15

Day 5—The Separation 17

Day 6—The Day 19

Day 7—Heaven 21

Day 8—The Nations 23

Day 9—The Seed 25

Day 10—The Lights 27

Day 11—Life 29

Day 12—Fruitfulness 31

Day 13—Diversity 33

Day 14—The Crown 35

Day 15—Authority 37

Day 16—Unity 39

Day 17—The Commission 41

Day 18—The Sabbath 45

Day 19—God and Man 47

Day 20—Labor 51

Day 21—The Test 53

Day 22—Fellowship 57

Day 23—Marriage 59

Day 24—Leaving and Cleaving 61

Day 25—Openness 63

Day 26—The Question 65

Day 27—The Trap 69

Day 28—The Deception 71

Day 29—The Fall 73

Day 30—The Cover Up 75

Day 31—The Delusion 77

Day 32—Fear 79

Day 33—The Voices 83

Day 34—The Fall Deepens 85

Day 35—The Curse on the Serpent 87

Day 36—The Curse on the Woman 91

Day 37—The Curse on the Man 93

Day 38—The Covering 97

Day 39—The Exile 99

Day 40—The Offering 103

Day 41—Sin and Depression 105

Day 42—Jealousy and Murder 107

Day 43—The Curse from the Ground 111

Day 44—Departing from the Lord 115

Day 45—They Called Upon the Lord 119

Day 46—Walking With God 123

Day 47—Noah and the Nephilim 125

Day 48—The Judgment 129

Day 49—The Covenant 133

Day 50—From Babylon to Abraham 137

Introduction

This daily devotional is designed to establish and strengthen the foundations of your spiritual life in fifty days. These foundations include our personal relationship to God, our relationship to His people, our relationship to the world, and the foundation for a deep and accurate understanding of the Scriptures. This could be summed up as loving the Lord, loving our neighbors, and growing in the knowledge of His ways.

The best place to start anything is at the beginning. Therefore, I have begun this study in Genesis. Genesis is so deep in its revelation of the Lord and His ways that if we studied it for a lifetime we could not exhaust it. There seems to be no end to the layer after layer of understanding that can be mined from just the first two chapters. In Genesis, the gospel message is foretold, as well as its glorious conclusion in the kingdom age in which Christ will return to rule and restore the earth. From this extraordinary foundation, the rest of the Scriptures are built, revealing the glorious and unfathomable ways of our God.

Our primary quest is to know the Lord and His ways. If we know Him, we will love Him. The more we know Him, the more we will be captured by the glory of who He is. We cannot help but to love His creation too, because His creation is a reflection of His nature. Our love will also grow for the crowning glory of His creation, man. Even though man's glory is now marred because of sin and rebellion, God made man in His own image, and we can see Him in every person if we know where to look. Then we begin to love mankind with a deeper, more effective love. This is a love that calls the fallen back to their high destiny in His plan for their lives.

I must also emphasize that even though I have sought to understand and convey a deeper, figurative meaning to the creation, this does not negate the fact that the creation story told in Genesis, is both a literal and factual account of how the Lord created the universe. Both the Law and the Prophets also apply metaphors and figurative meanings to literal events, and I have endeavored to remain within the guidelines that Scripture itself sets. All of the metaphors used in

Genesis are also found elsewhere in Scripture, and their meanings are well established.

Even so, we should also be careful not to use the metaphors of Scripture for establishing doctrine. We should instead use them as powerful tools for illuminating and confirming the sound doctrines that are clearly and literally established in the Scriptures. It was in this sense that King David recognized that the incense offered to the Lord in His tabernacle represented prayer (Psalm 141:2). Also, the apostle Paul recognized that the mothers of Ishmael and Isaac represented the two covenants (Galatians 4:24). We should ask: If these two women in Genesis allegorically represented something as profound as the two covenants, how much more does the rest of the story represent?

However, there is a danger in approaching Scripture seeking to understand its allegorical meaning. One of the primary traps is to use "free association" in the interpretation of Scripture. This gives the liberty to make the Scriptures say just about anything we want them to say, which is a foundation for error. We do not want them to say what we want, but what the Lord intended. The Scriptures speak allegorically, but to understand the allegories properly, we must first have a deep commitment to the literal interpretation, and then allow the Scriptures themselves to point to any allegorical interpretation.

For example, as David implied that incense represented prayer in Psalm 141, we can see how Moses also understood this. Therefore, when a plague began to sweep the camp of Israel after Korah's rebellion, he directed Aaron to run into the midst of the camp with incense to stop the plague (see Numbers 16). This is a message to all generations that prayer can stop the plagues that are killing people.

The understanding we gain is not just so we can enjoy a deeper faith in God's plan for ourselves, but is to enable us to be used more effectively in His great plan. The more light we have, the more we should be carriers of that light to those who are bound in darkness.

We are told in I Corinthians 2:10, **"For to us God revealed them through the Spirit; for the Spirit searches all things, even the depths of God."** If we have the Holy Spirit, there will be a yearning within us to search the depths of God's ways, to sink our roots deeper into His truth, and to draw closer to Him. If we are drawing closer to Him, and abiding in Him, we will also bear more fruit.

Knowledge without works produces an arrogance that is contrary to His nature. Knowledge combined with the true work of the Spirit produces humility. Therefore, since we only know in part, we are always searching for more of Him. This is my prayer for you as you go through this study, that it would produce in you an unquenchable thirst for more of God, and a deeper knowledge of His ways.

Please excuse the few redundant Scripture references and insights that are occasionally used. These are repeated purposely in order to aid retention, and sometimes for linkage with previous thoughts.

If there is one overall message that I hope to convey through this devotional, it is that just as the days of creation were full of purpose and the revelation of God, every day of our lives should be the same. We read in **Exodus 16:4:**

> **Then the LORD said to Moses, "Behold, I will rain bread from heaven for you; and the people shall go out and gather a day's portion every day, that I may test them, whether or not they will walk in My instruction."**

This is still a test for all who would follow God. Will we gather fresh "bread from heaven" every day? The true God seekers will be so addicted to Him that their first thought every morning will be that they must seek Him, and have a fresh revelation of Him for the day. As the Lord Himself said in Matthew 4:4: **"It is written, 'Man shall not live on bread alone, but on every word that proceeds out of the mouth of God.'"** Note that this is not a word that *proceeded* from the mouth of God, but that *proceeds*. This speaks of the present, fresh word that comes from Him daily. We really cannot live spiritually without it.

DAY 1

The Beginning

In the beginning God created the heavens and the earth (Genesis 1:1).

Understanding the beginning is the beginning of understanding. The first verse in the Bible may include the four most important words ever written—*"in the beginning God."* The understanding of this one verse is the foundation upon which all truth is based. Before we can comprehend the end of the age, or our present purposes, we must first understand the beginning. This is the foundation upon which everything else is built.

"In the beginning GOD...," these four words are worthy of a lifetime of study, and will be the basis upon which an eternity of worship will be founded. We exist because of God. We, therefore, owe Him everything. He alone is worthy of our worship and devotion.

At the end of the age, the most pressing philosophical controversies still revolve around our origin. This is understandable because when we answer this one question right, the answers to all other questions are possible. If we answer it wrong, the door opens to almost every form of darkness and deception.

Just as the strength of a foundation will determine the magnitude of what can be built upon it, the depth to which we understand this one truth about our origin can determine the spiritual strength of our entire life. When we understand that we had our beginning in God, and that He made us for His purposes, we are compelled to return to Him. The truth of our beginning is also the beginning of all truth. Since He made us, we are His. Therefore, His purpose and His plan must guide us.

If God made us, then we can no longer claim to be the centers of this universe. He is the center. Jesus is the Alpha and the Omega, the Beginning and the End. He is *I Am*. All things will be summed up in Him. Just as every compass will point to the magnetic north, all else will ultimately point to Him, the magnetic pole of truth. With this pole of truth in our hearts, we have a basis for every decision—what is His will? All things came from Him and all will return to Him. This is our destiny and the goal of our lives—to return to the One who made us, and to serve Him in all things.

Also implied is the importance of all beginnings. How we begin our day will probably determine the quality of our day. How we begin our marriages will have a lot to do with the quality of our marriages. How we begin our jobs, ministries, or any other venture, will determine their foundations. How something is started is often the primary factor in the quality of what is finished. Projects begun on an impulse are just as quickly and easily abandoned. For any significant project that is accomplished, great care must be taken while laying the foundation.

The foundation is the single part of any building that is used every day. If it collapses, the rest of the building will collapse. The apostle Paul wrote in I Corinthians 3:11, **"For no man can lay a foundation other than the one which is laid, which is Jesus Christ."** Knowing Jesus and abiding in Him is the foundation of our spiritual lives. We may build many things upon this foundation, and we may learn many great truths about His ways and His purposes. We may do great things for Him, but coming to Him every day, and doing all that we do with Him instead of just for Him, is essential if we are to bear true spiritual fruit. Paul also wrote in Ephesians 1:9-10:

> **He made known to us the mystery of His will, according to His kind intention which He purposed in Him**
> **with a view to an administration suitable to the fulness of the times, that is, the summing up of all things in Christ, things in the heavens and things upon the earth. In Him.**

The ultimate purpose of God is that all things will be summed up in His Son. If we do not keep the ultimate purpose of God as the focus of our lives, and assure that all we do is founded in Him, we will continually be distracted by the lesser purposes of God. Many are distracted from the River of Life by the little tributaries that feed it. If you want to stay in the River, keep your focus on Jesus Christ in all things. No other foundation can be laid that will stand.

DAY 2

The Plan

And the earth was formless and void, and darkness was over the surface of the deep (Genesis 1:2).

The Hebrew word that is translated "without form" is *tohuw* (to'-hoo), which is defined as "a desolation, desert." In the KJV this word is also translated "confusion, empty place, nothing." The point is that the Holy Spirit can make a glorious creation out of the most desolate place. He can also bring forth a glorious new creation out of the most desolate, confused, and empty life.

The most important step in any journey is the first one. If we are going to get where we are going, we must know where we are. The Lord also seems to delight in beginning with that which is formless and void. Or, we could say, He likes to start with a clean canvas. One of the most wonderful truths of Christianity is that when we come to Him, we are born again, and all things become new. Part of the good news of the gospel is that in Christ we can start all over. We do not just start a few things over, but everything! When the power of His cross begins to work in our lives, we are redeemed, and the power of redemption flows through us to redeem everything in our lives.

Some translators have rendered "formless and void" in Genesis 1:2 as "chaos." That too, has an important application. If the Holy Spirit took the earth that was in such chaos, and brought forth a creation of such beauty and symmetry, He can do the same with any life that is offered to Him. Regardless of how much chaos our lives are in, He not only will straighten it all out, He will make it glorious.

By watching the Holy Spirit bring order and new beginnings to lives, we can learn much about the Lord and His ways. Even though we begin again afresh, let us not make the same mistake of thinking that we have the wisdom and knowledge to do it right. When we are born again, we come to know our complete dependence upon our Creator. This alone will enable us to avoid the traps ahead so that we do not fall again to the same mistakes. The apostle Paul stated:

For consider your calling, brethren, that there were not many wise according to the flesh, not many mighty, not many noble;

but God has chosen the foolish things of the world to shame the wise, and God has chosen the weak things of the world to shame the things which are strong,

and the base things of the world and the despised, God has chosen, the things that are not, that He might nullify the things that are, that no man should boast before God (I Corinthians 1:26-29).

Every fresh new move of God in church history began with those who really did not know what they were doing or where they were going. Like Abraham, they had to leave the country that had form and substance, to seek God in a place that was still formless and void of definition. Just as Paul had to be struck blind in the natural so that he could see in the spirit, we too must become void of our own vision before we will look to Him. However, the Lord does not leave us in this state, but begins to show us what He is building. Then He can give us the plans for the mansion He wants us to add to the glorious city that He is building.

At the beginning of our journey, we must understand that we are not just taking a random course, but it is a part of His plan for us. Everything seems to be formless and void at first, but as we follow the moving of His Spirit, a beautiful creation, our new life in Him, starts to take shape. In fact, God's plan for us is so comprehensive that He knew us before the foundation of the world, and our calling was known at that time. The foundation of our purpose is for us to become conformed to the image of Jesus Christ—that we become like Him and do the works that He did. This calling is upon every believer. He has also given each of us a very specific part to play in His overall plan. It must be our quest to search for our part in His plan.

Abraham may not have known where he was going, but he did know what he was looking for. He left everything to be a part of what God was building. This is also our quest, to be a part of what God is doing.

DAY 3

The Spirit Moves

And the Spirit of God was moving over the surface of the waters (Genesis 1:2).

With the first mention of the Spirit, He was moving. The Holy Spirit is the agent of God who does the work. He is ever moving, working, and bringing forth the purposes of God. It is crucial for every Christian to know the Holy Spirit, and learn how to follow Him in all things. In order to do this, we have to keep moving. The nature of the Christian life is to be moving and going somewhere.

The Christian life is never stagnant, but flowing like a river. We have a destination and a work to accomplish with the Holy Spirit. In the beginning **"the Spirit of God was moving,"** and the Spirit continues to move. That is why the River of Life is a river, not a pond or lake. A river is always going somewhere.

A river starts as a single drop of water, and then becomes a little stream. Next, the stream gathers with other streams from the country side, and the river grows until it reaches its destination. The Lord intends this for every life. We are called to a journey that grows continually in both life and power. If we stay on the course, Proverbs 4:18 will be true of us: **"But the path of the righteous is like the light of dawn, that shines brighter and brighter until the full day."**

We all begin as a single drop, a single soul among the teaming billions on earth. Then, **"if we walk in the light as He Himself is in the light, we have fellowship with one another" (I John 1:7).** Our journey is not alone. There is no other fellowship on earth like that which is found in the church of Jesus Christ. We are called to walk with other souls. If we stay on course, we will gather with many others who are going to the same destination. Our little streams should then join others, growing all of the time into a mighty river. The church is also a glorious gift. Each soul is a marvelous treasure to be discovered.

When the Spirit moved, life came forth. The formless void became a symphony of such harmony and beauty, that we will for eternity continue to marvel at the wonder of His ways. The Holy Spirit still loves to take even the most desolate life and turn it into a glorious symphony of life. However, He also builds with permanence. Our God planned from eternity, and as King Solomon understood: **"I know that everything God does will remain forever; there is nothing to add to it and there is nothing to take from it, for God has so worked that men should fear Him" (Ecclesiastes 3:14).** To the degree that we work in harmony with His plan, we will be used to do that which will last forever. This is called "having fruit that remains."

The church is the "new creation" of God. When we look at the beginning of the church, we are observing a second beginning with consequences no less profound than the first beginning. When the spiritual state of the earth was formless and void, the Spirit moved again and the church was born. All life springs from the Spirit of God, and we will only have true life when we learn to move with Him. As we behold His work, we learn never to be discouraged by the present state of things. The more desolate they are, the more glorious His work appears.

If our spiritual lives are not getting better day by day, and increasing in life and power, then somewhere we have missed a turn. If this is true for you, do not proceed any further along your present course, but return to your first love, your personal relationship with Jesus Christ. There you will find the Living Waters that can alone satisfy your soul and lead you to your destiny. Do not let petty differences with others separate you from those whose destiny is joined to your own. This is how many turn from the course. Stay in the River.

The Christian life is one of movement. However, it is not a random movement, but one with purpose. This purpose is still turning that which is formless and void into a glorious new creation. If we allow the Spirit to move through us, we will also be constantly searching for those whose lives are formless and void. We will become a bridge for them into the glorious, creative purposes of God.

When we begin to see with His eyes, we will not see any person or situation as worthless, regardless of how empty and useless they may now seem. When we begin to see with His eyes, we begin to see potential in people and situations that before were seemingly hopeless. He said in Jeremiah 15:19: **"If you return, then I will restore you— Before Me you will stand; and if you extract the precious from the worthless, you will become My spokesman."**

DAY 4

The Light

Then God said, "Let there be light"; and there was light (Genesis 1:3).

Without light, we could not see. Light makes all things manifest. After the Spirit moved, His first great task was to bring forth light. Light represents truth, and as soon as the Lord begins to move in our lives, His first task will be to shine the light of His truth into our lives.

It is interesting to note, that light was created before the sun, moon, and the stars, and did not take place until the fourth "day" of creation. Light was created before the vessels that were to manifest it. Jesus is the Light of the world, and He existed as One with God before the world. We see this in John's great explanation of Jesus at the beginning of His gospel:

In the beginning was the Word, and the Word was with God, and the Word was God.
He was in the beginning with God.
All things came into being by Him, and apart from Him nothing came into being that has come into being.
In Him was life, and the life was the light of men.
There was the true light which, coming into the world, enlightens every man.
He was in the world, and the world was made through Him, and the world did not know Him.
He came to His own, and those who were His own did not receive Him.
But as many as received Him, to them He gave the right to become children of God, even to those who believe in His name (John 1:1-4, 9-12).

Jesus was the plan of God from the beginning. He is the Son who makes His Father's heart glad. In everything that was created the Father looks for the reflection of His Son, and in everything that was created there is a message about the Son, as Paul explained in Colossians 1:16-17:

For by Him all things were created, both in the heavens and on earth, visible and invisible, whether thrones or dominions or rulers or authorities—all things have been created by Him and for Him.

And He is before all things, and in Him all things hold together.

"**In Him all things hold together**" reveals that He is the binding force in all of creation. The light was created before the sun, moon, and stars as an eternal testimony that He must be given first place in everything. Every new believer needs to be saturated with the revelation of whom Jesus is before their attention is turned to all of the other doctrines of the faith, or an understanding of their place in the church. The Light, Jesus, must have preeminence in all things. He is the first, and He is the last. Jesus is the Light of God, and all things will be summed up in Him. We must know Him first.

As we read before in I John 1:7, "**but if we walk in the light as He Himself is in the light, we have fellowship with one another.**" This scripture makes clear, if we depart from fellowship, we also depart from His light. If we break fellowship with His people, we will also be breaking fellowship with Him. Christianity without fellowship is not true Christianity. The Lord created His church so we would all need one another. No one will get to their destination in Christ alone.

Church life can be one of the most glorious, and most difficult, experiences we can have. Amos 3:3 states, "**Can two walk together, except they be agreed?**" **(KJV)** This does not imply that we must agree on everything to walk together, but we walk together in the things upon which we do agree. Every Christian agrees that Jesus Christ is Lord, so every Christian can walk together to some degree. There should be at least some level of fellowship between all who hold to the basic truths of the faith.

As we walk together, understanding and agreement will grow. To have fellowship, we must start by looking for things upon which we agree, rather than those upon which we disagree. This will enable us to stay in the light, which requires that we "**have fellowship with one another**" **(I John 1:7)**. Likewise, when we start breaking off fellowship with God's people, we will start walking in darkness. We cannot be joined to Jesus Christ without also being joined to His body, the church.

DAY 5

The Separation

And God saw that the light was good; and God separated the light from the darkness. And God called the light day, and the darkness He called night (Genesis 1:4-5).

Yesterday, we discussed the fellowship and union that we have with the Lord and other Christians. At the same time the Lord is joining us to Himself and His people, He will also be separating us from the darkness in our lives, and those who walk in darkness. This is a necessary process if we are to abide in Christ Jesus.

After we come to know Jesus as the Light, God begins to separate the light from the darkness in our lives. This can be a difficult time because it is easy to become so distracted by the darkness that we lose sight of the Light. It is crucial for us to always keep our attention on the Lord, who is our Light, even when the Holy Spirit is convicting us of sin, or revealing people or situations that we must avoid.

Darkness represents sin. The light will immediately begin to reveal the sin in our lives. Even small matters that we never thought about before, such as telling little lies, suddenly become dark and ugly. There will be a strong tendency at this point to just turn the light off. When we come to understand the grotesque nature of all sin, the exposure of that sin can seem intolerable. We must either turn the light off and go back to our old lives, or remove the sin. There can be no compromise. If we are to proceed, light and darkness must be separated. The Lord Jesus said,

But I tell you the truth, it is to your advantage that I go away; for if I do not go away, the Helper shall not come to you; but if I go, I will send Him to you.
And He, when He comes, will convict the world concerning sin, and righteousness, and judgment (John 16:7-8).

When the Holy Spirit moves, He always convicts us of sin, but He also reveals the counter to our sin which is righteousness. Then He will

17

show us the consequences of sin, which is judgment. It is hard, but it is essential before the new creation can begin to bloom in our lives. When we are confronted with the realization of the depth of our sin, we are compelled to cast ourselves upon the mercy of God at the cross. We can only find peace at the cross of Jesus, and there He becomes our Savior. His cross becomes the peace and joy of our lives. It is a hard work to have our sin exposed, but we have relief and comfort at the cross. Always flee to the cross!

There is deliverance from the darkness in our lives. When we see the darkness, the light becomes even brighter. We must see the darkness and how utterly dark our sins are, but the purpose in the darkness being exposed is to separate us from it. Therefore, we must not become overly focused on the darkness, but turn immediately to the light. We are told in II Corinthians 3:18:

But we all, with unveiled face beholding as in a mirror, the glory of the Lord, are being transformed into the same image from glory to glory, just as from the Lord, the Spirit.

We must see our sin in order to repent. We are not changed by seeing our sin, but by turning to the Lord and by seeing His glory. Whenever our sin is exposed, we must repent, then quickly turn to the Lord and His righteousness. Our goal is not to become perfect people, but to abide in the One who is perfect. Our righteousness will never be in us, but will always be in Him. It is not what we do, but what He has already done, that changes us.

If we start focusing on the darkness in our lives, we will fall into a black hole that is very difficult to escape. Do not look for darkness in your life, but allow the Holy Spirit to shine the light on it. When He exposes the darkness, He will also give us the truth that sets us free. Our goal must always be to keep our attention on the light, and let the light expose whatever darkness is in our lives. See it, repent of it, and then keep following the light.

As we follow the light, much of the darkness will separate from us automatically, which is why Jesus said love was the fulfillment of the Law. If we will follow the two simple commandments, to love the Lord and to love our neighbors, we will fulfill the whole Law. If we love the Lord, we will not worship idols, etc. If we love our neighbors, we will not murder, envy what is theirs, or steal from them. As we grow in the light of God's love, the darkness will be exposed and separate from us. Follow love, and you will follow the Light.

DAY 6

The Day

And there was evening and there was morning, one day (Genesis 1:5).

Here we see that a day begins with the evening. This is a prophecy that with the great things the Lord brings forth, there is usually darkness before the dawn. This is a consistent truth throughout the Scriptures.

For example, Israel was subject to four hundred years of slavery before they were led into the freedom of the Promised Land. Their oppression became the greatest just before they were set free by the power of God. The great saints of Scripture usually went through a period of darkness before they were brought forth into the purposes of God. Joseph had to go through slavery and imprisonment. King David was persecuted by Saul, and chased by the very people over which he was called to rule. Jesus had to go to the cross and die before He could be resurrected to His place of authority and glory.

Between the place where we receive the promises of God and the fulfillment of those promises, there will almost always be a wilderness that is the exact opposite of what we have been promised. In order to test their faith and purify their hearts, the children of Israel had to wander through a desert, where there was no water, before they could get to the Promised Land flowing with milk and honey. We will go through trials too. Even so, as we are told in James 1:2-4,12:

Consider it all joy, my brethren, when you encounter various trials,

knowing that the testing of your faith produces endurance.

And let endurance have its perfect result, that you may be perfect and complete, lacking in nothing.

Blessed is a man who perseveres under trial; for once he has been approved, he will receive the crown of life, which the Lord has promised to those who love Him.

Every trial in our lives is allowed for two purposes. The first is to conform us to the image of Jesus Christ, which is the fruit of the Spirit. The second is to bring us to a place of maturity where He can trust us with more authority to do the works that He did, which are through the gifts of the Spirit. Therefore, we must seize our trials as James encourages, counting them as joy, because they always lead to the dawn's light. We also have the great promise in I Corinthians 10:13:

No temptation has overtaken you but such as is common to man; and God is faithful, who will not allow you to be tempted beyond what you are able, but with the temptation will provide the way of escape also, that you may be able to endure it.

God is the One allowing the temptation, and He is also in control, so we are never tempted beyond what we are able to endure. Therefore, when it gets so hard that we are getting close to the limit of what we can take, we should also know we are getting close to the end of the trial.

We are also assured that there is a way of escape with every trial. The way of escape is always the same, and that is the cross. If we would go to the cross and die to ourselves, our own ambitions, and the cares of this world, which are usually the roots of our trials, we would immediately find a peace that goes beyond human understanding. We are called to be dead to this world (see Galatians 6:14). What can the world do to a dead man? It is impossible for a dead man to feel rejected, abused, taken advantage of, or be concerned with loss. If we would go to the cross daily with all that we are and have, we would be the most free people the world has ever seen.

If we would go to the cross and die to our own interests every day, we would also be free to love without reservation. Love that is not self-centered is not controlled by the fear of pain or loss. Neither does this love try to control the object of our love.

Just as there could be no resurrection without there first being a death; there can be no victory without a battle. Like the tests we take in school to go on to higher levels, every test we endure in our lives is so we can go on to higher levels of maturity in the Lord. We should see every test as a great opportunity. The greater the test, the greater the opportunity. Always remember that regardless of how dark it seems to get, the light will certainly come, just as surely as the sun will rise every day.

DAY 7

Heaven

Then God said, "Let there be an expanse in the midst of the waters, and let it separate the waters from the waters."

And God made the expanse, and separated the waters which were below the expanse from the waters which were above the expanse; and it was so.

And God called the expanse heaven. And there was evening and there was morning, a second day (Genesis 1:6-8).

Immediately after we start the process of separating the light from the darkness in our lives, we must look up and begin to see the expanse of heaven. Heaven is not a fairy tale, nor a carrot on a stick that the Lord uses to make us be good. It is more real than the physical universe, and heaven is above the physical universe. Neither is heaven beyond the farthest galaxy. It is a realm in our very midst, and one which we can see and begin to experience now, as we are told in Ephesians:

Blessed be the God and Father of our Lord Jesus Christ, who has blessed us with every spiritual blessing in the heavenly places in Christ (Ephesians 1:3)

But God, being rich in mercy, because of His great love with which He loved us,

even when we were dead in our transgressions, made us alive together with Christ (by grace you have been saved),

and raised us up with Him, and seated us with Him in the heavenly places, in Christ Jesus (Ephesians 2:4-6).

At the very time we are struggling with the darkness that manifests in our lives, we begin to see both how dead we are in our transgressions, and how the Father has raised and seated us with His Son in the heavenly places. As we behold the glory of the heavenlies, where Christ is seated, far above all rule, authority, and power, we know we have been placed with Him by the power of His cross, not by our own righteousness. We do not just cover the darkness in our lives, but instead we must rise above it into a new and ever expanding glory.

The earthly minded will constantly try to restrain those who are seekers of God with such statements as, "Don't become so heavenly minded that you are no earthly good," which is precisely the opposite of true wisdom. Heaven is the realm into which we are called to abide with Christ Jesus, and the only truly effective ministry we will ever have on this earth is originated from that position. The church that becomes too earthly minded is not doing the earth any good. We are called to be a bridge between heaven and earth, and to represent the reality of all we have been given in Christ Jesus in the heavenly places. Christians should be so saturated with heaven that it is more real to them than anything in the natural realm. Only then will we reveal the light that is more powerful than any darkness, and begin to call the earth out of her terrible night into the dawning light of Christ.

word Search

"From that time Jesus began to preach and say, "Repent, for the kingdom of heaven is at hand" (Matthew 4:17). The entire message that Jesus preached on the earth was centered around His teachings on **"the kingdom of heaven."** Most of His teachings began with **"the kingdom of heaven is like..."** If we are to understand the message of Jesus, it is fundamental that we understand the kingdom of heaven.

The apostle John recorded in Revelation 4:1: **"After these things I looked, and behold, a door standing open in heaven, and the first voice which I had heard, like the sound of a trumpet speaking with me, said, "Come up here, and I will show you what must take place after these things."** That voice is still calling to all who will hear. There is a door open in heaven and the Spirit is beckoning us to come up there. The ultimate quest of every Christian is to walk the earth from a position seated with Christ Jesus in the heavenly places.

Therefore, our prayer must be the one that He taught His disciples, for His kingdom to come, and His will to be done, on earth as it is in heaven (see Matthew 6:10). We can never be too heavenly minded. The true good that we are able to do on earth will be dependent on the degree to which we have attained the heavenly treasures. We must always keep our devotion to obey Matthew 6:33, **"But seek first His kingdom and His righteousness; and all these things shall be added to you."**

Day 8

The Nations

Then God said, "Let the waters below the heavens be gathered into one place, and let the dry land appear"; and it was so.

And God called the dry land earth, and the gathering of the waters He called seas; and God saw that it was good (Genesis 1:9-10).

In Scripture, seas often represent nations, as we see in Isaiah 17:12: **"Alas, the uproar of many peoples who roar like the roaring of the seas, and the rumbling of nations who rush on like the rumbling of mighty waters!"** This is also seen in Revelation 17:15: **And he said to me, "The waters which you saw where the harlot sits, are peoples and multitudes and nations and tongues.**

In the previous verses in Genesis, the Lord established the heavens. Immediately after this, He established the seas, which represent nations. As Paul explained in I Corinthians 15:46-49:

However, the spiritual is not first, but the natural; then the spiritual.

The first man is from the earth, earthy; the second man is from heaven.

As is the earthy, so also are those who are earthy; and as is the heavenly, so also are those who are heavenly.

And just as we have borne the image of the earthy, we shall also bear the image of the heavenly.

The new creation follows the same pattern as the original creation. Immediately after we have our place established with Christ Jesus seated in the heavenly places, He then wants to give us a vision for the nations (seas). As was written concerning the Son in Psalms 2:8: **"Ask of me, and I will surely give the nations as Thine inheritance, and the very ends of the earth as Thy possession."** The church is the Lord's bride, but the nations are His inheritance. He created the nations, the different cultures and peoples, and they each have a specific, and glorious, purpose in Him. The Great Commission was:

"Go therefore and make disciples of all nations, baptizing them in the name of the Father and the Son and the Holy Spirit,

teaching them to observe all that I commanded you; and lo, I am with you always, even to the end of the age" (Matthew 28:19-20).

We were not saved just so we can sit in the heavens, but so we can go forth with the glorious message of the cross. We need to be firmly established with the Lord and His authority before we go, but then we do need to go. If we do not live with a mission in our life, we will be counted with the backsliders, or old wineskins. Our love for the Lord compels us to see that He will receive the reward for His sacrifice—the nations.

When the Lord finished separating the water into seas, which represent the nations, He said that it was "good." God obviously loves the diversity of different cultures and nations. He has deposited unique gifts in each one which reflects His own nature. The first response of those who love the blessed Creator, when meeting those who are different, should be the expectation of a deeper revelation of the Lord's ways through them. Our differences are not meant to contradict and conflict with each other, but rather to compliment one another. As the Scripture teaches, even those with the gift of prophecy only see in part. To see the whole picture, we must put our part together with what He has given to others. To have an accurate view, we need each other. After the Lord divided the waters into different seas, He said that it was a "good" thing.

Loving diversity is one of the basic natures of God. However, this is one of His basic characteristics that much of the church has tended to neglect. The pressure toward conformity is not from God. He loves diversity. Accordingly, those who know the Creator should be the most creative, and free people on earth.

It was for freedom that Christ set us free; therefore keep standing firm and do not be subject again to a yoke of slavery (Galatians 5:1).

DAY 9

The Seed

Then God said, "Let the earth sprout vegetation, plants yielding seed, and fruit trees bearing fruit after their kind, with seed in them, on the earth"; and it was so.

And the earth brought forth vegetation, plants yielding seed after their kind, and trees bearing fruit, with seed in them, after their kind; and God saw that it was good.

And there was evening and there was morning, a third day (Genesis 1:11-13).

The basic understanding of both the old and new creation begins with understanding the seed. As stated yesterday, the Lord loves diversity, and to protect and preserve it, He created seeds that would only bear fruit after their own kind. Every plant has a role to play in the balance of creation. If a plant or animal was to lose its uniqueness, it could not play its role, and the balance that enables life as we know it on this wonderful planet would begin to erode. Knowing this very well, one of the basic strategies of the enemy is to destroy life and to blur the distinctions that God created. Fully accomplished, this alone could undermine and unravel the harmony of the creation that is necessary to support life.

If life is to go on, the basic differences between men and women cannot be compromised. The way a man and a woman become one is not by the man becoming a woman or the woman becoming a man, but by the recognition and appreciation of the differences. If this appreciation ever ceased, the human race would end. The reason the Lord created every seed to bear fruit **"after its own kind,"** was so the uniqueness that perpetuates life would continue.

As the Lord explained in The Parable of the Sower, words are also seeds. Seeds grow up to become plants that bear fruit. What is growing from our words? What will the fruit of our words be like? If we speak out of bitterness, we are planting bitter fruit in the earth. If our words are filled with faith, hope, or love, we are planting trees that will one day bear the fruit of faith, hope, and love in the earth.

I live in the highlands of North Carolina. On our mountain there are thousands of apple trees. Apples were supposedly brought to this region by Johnny Appleseed. He used to say, "Any man can count the seeds in an apple, but only God can count the apples in a seed." No one seems to know how many apple seeds he planted in our area, but now, two hundred years later, there are millions of apples harvested each fall. Like seeds, our words also take time to sprout. We may not even be here to see the fruit of them. And like seeds, words are very likely to multiply. Let us consider each day that our words will bear fruit, and determine we will only sow that which brings forth the fruit of the Spirit.

The Lord also compared faith to a seed. Jesus told His disciples that if they had the faith as a grain of mustard seed, they could move mountains (see Matthew 17:20). History testifies that there is no force on earth that can stop true faith. The disciples not only moved mountains, they moved nations and empires. They understood the principle of the seed. If even the seed could move mountains, what could the full plant do?

Just as the wise King Solomon wrote in Proverbs 18:21: **"Death and life are in the power of the tongue, and those who love it will eat its fruit."** Let us be sure the fruit of our words will be something we will want to eat. Are our words imparting life or death? Are they building people's faith or feeding their fears? Are they bringing forth love and reconciliation, or division and strife? Remember, whatever the fruit is bearing, we ourselves will have to eat it eventually. We are told in Ephesians 4:29-32:

> **Let no unwholesome word proceed from your mouth, but only such a word as is good for edification according to the need of the moment, that it may give grace to those who hear.**
>
> **And do not grieve the Holy Spirit of God, by whom you were sealed for the day of redemption.**
>
> **Let all bitterness and wrath and anger and clamor and slander be put away from you, along with all malice.**
>
> **And be kind to one another, tender-hearted, forgiving each other, just as God in Christ also has forgiven you.**

According to this scripture, a primary way we can grieve the Holy Spirit is by letting unwholesome words come from our mouths such as those from bitterness, wrath, anger, etc. Let us determine that we will not sow these seeds, but rather always speak words which will edify and build up one another.

DAY 10

The Lights

> Then God said, "Let there be lights in the expanse of the heavens to separate the day from the night, and let them be for signs, and for seasons, and for days and years;
>
> and let them be for lights in the expanse of the heavens to give light on the earth"; and it was so.
>
> And God made the two great lights, the greater light to govern the day, and the lesser light to govern the night; He made the stars also.
>
> And God placed them in the expanse of the heavens to give light on the earth,
>
> and to govern the day and the night, and to separate the light from the darkness; and God saw that it was good.
>
> And there was evening and there was morning, a fourth day (Genesis 1:14-19).

The sun is the power which makes all life possible on the earth. Therefore, it is often used in Scripture to represent Jesus, who is likewise the source of all life as we read in Colossians 1:16-17: **"For by Him all things were created, both in the heavens and on earth, visible and invisible, whether thrones or dominions or rulers or authorities—all things have been created by Him and for Him. And He is before all things, and in Him all things hold together."** The Lord Jesus was with the Father before the foundation of the world, and was the Creator of the world as we see in John 1:1-4,10:

> In the beginning was the Word, and the Word was with God, and the Word was God.
>
> He was in the beginning with God.
>
> All things came into being by Him, and apart from Him nothing came into being that has come into being.
>
> In Him was life, and the life was the light of men.
>
> He was in the world, and the world was made through Him, and the world did not know Him.

Jesus is not only the One through whom all things were made, He is everything that the Father loves. In every thing created, He was looking for the likeness of His Son. He is looking for His Son in us. To know Him is to know the Father and have eternal life. Just as the sun is the source of our physical life, and life on earth would perish instantly if the sun went dark, so Jesus is the source of all life. Even those who do not know Him cannot live a moment without Him.

The moon represents the church, which is not the source of light, but reflects the light of the sun. Just as the moon rules the night, the church age has been a dark time for mankind. Yet in spite of all of her flaws and mistakes, the church has given light to the nations. Just as the gravitational pull of the moon controls the tides, the church has had enough pull over the nations to be a great influence of the events in this age. However, she is not the Light, and can never rule over the nations until the Light Himself returns. The church's purpose in this age is to give enough light to those who will use it to make it through the night.

Stars in Scripture often represent messengers. The Lord explained that the seven stars which He held in His hand represented the angels of the seven churches (see Revelation 1:20). The Greek word translated "angels" is *aggelos* (ang'-el-os), which literally means a "messenger." This word sometimes denoted angelic messengers, but often represented a person, especially apostles who were the special messengers of the New Testament. This is generally understood to be the meaning of these "stars" in Revelation, because the words given to the seven churches were to be delivered to the "angel" of each church (see Revelation 1:11-20). Because angelic messengers did not need to have such words delivered to them in writing, these "stars" have always been considered the leaders of each of these churches.

As stars are used for navigation at night, the Lord has been faithful to send His messengers to the world to help men navigate through the darkness. Messengers have come and helped steer the course of history, but we must always keep in mind that all men are "lesser lights," as we always seek to walk in the greater light of Christ. When the sun rises, the stars disappear. Likewise, when the Lord returns in His glory we will not be so impressed by any man, even the greatest spiritual leaders. However, while there is still darkness, we need those who have been sent with a little light to help us through the times. It is right that we honor our spiritual leaders, knowing that they have been sent to help us stay on course. When the Son arises and the day dawns with the full light of Christ, we will not need spiritual leaders, but until that time we certainly do.

DAY 11

Life

Then God said, "Let the waters teem with swarms of living creatures, and let birds fly above the earth in the open expanse of the heavens."

And God created the great sea monsters, and every living creature that moves, with which the waters swarmed after their kind, and every winged bird after its kind; and God saw that it was good (Genesis 1:20-21).

The Lord said that His people were worth **"more than many sparrows,"** (**Matthew 10:31**) so sparrows are obviously worth something to Him. When He created the beasts He **"saw that it was good" (Genesis 1:25).** The creation is precious to the Lord, which is why we see in Revelation 11:18 that when the Lord's great wrath comes at the end, one reason is **"to destroy those who destroy the earth."** Christians should be the most devoted conservationists of all, counting precious what our wonderful Creator has given us to enjoy on the earth. Life, in all of its forms, must be esteemed and protected. However, this must not be confused with the idolatrous worship of the creation in place of the Creator.

In John 10:10 the Lord said, **"I came that they might have life, and might have it abundantly."** He is called **"the Prince of life" (Acts 3:15).** He came to lead us in the path of life. In Him is life, and He is the One with the words of life. If we are abiding in Him, life should likewise be flowing from us. We have been given a well of living water that will never run dry. In all that we do, we should love, seek, preserve, and spread life.

One of the most ancient philosophical questions is: What is life? In simplified terms, life is communication. We have life for as long as we can communicate, or interrelate, with our environment. Man is called a "higher form of life" because we communicate on a higher level. We are likewise alive spiritually only if we communicate spiritually. As the Lord said in John 6:63, **"the words that I have spoken to you are**

spirit and are life." We only have spiritual life if we hear His words, or communicate on a spiritual level. If we are alive in the spirit, then they can kill our bodies but they cannot take our lives. As He said in John 11:25-26, **"I am the resurrection and the life; he who believes in Me shall live even if he dies, and everyone who lives and believes in Me shall never die."**

In Scripture, our spirit is sometimes referred to as our heart. That is why we read in Proverbs 4:23, **"Watch over your heart with all diligence, for from it flow the springs of life."** The Lord explained in Luke 6:45 that **"the good man out of the good treasure of his heart brings forth what is good; and the evil man out of the evil treasure brings forth what is evil; for his mouth speaks from that which fills his heart."** We quoted before from Proverbs 18:21, **"Death and life are in the power of the tongue, and those who love it will eat its fruit."** As a famous statesman once said, "Let your words be sweet because you never know when you may have to eat them!"

Our words are an indication of what is in our hearts. Proverbs 10:11 states, **"The mouth of the righteous is a fountain of life."** As James wrote, **"Does a fountain send out from the same opening both fresh and bitter water?" (James 3:11)** Amazing, but true, our words can actually have the power of life or death in them. The words of the gospel preached can actually have the seed of eternal life in them. Let us always guard our words so that they impart life.

The Lord loves life. He created the world to **"swarm"** with life. If we are in unity with Him, we will promote life in everything. Death is an enemy that has invaded the creation. Death will be defeated, but until its ultimate defeat, let us confront and overcome it with life. We should always consider how we can promote and protect life. Let us always speak words of life and hope, determining to overcome death with life by bearing fruit that remains. We should always be sure that our words are His words and are "spirit and life."

In Psalm 16:11 we read, **"Thou wilt make known to me the path of life; in Thy presence is fulness of joy."** The Lord Jesus is the Source of all life. The closer we are to Him, the more life we will have in us. As King David also wrote in Psalm 36:9, **"For with Thee is the fountain of life; in Thy light we see light."** Let us choose today to abide in the Source of all life, and let His life flow through us to bring life to others.

DAY 12

Fruitfulness

And God blessed them, saying, "Be fruitful and multiply, and fill the waters in the seas, and let birds multiply on the earth."

And there was evening and there was morning, a fifth day (Genesis 1:22-23).

The very first blessing the Lord pronounced over His creation was to be fruitful and multiply. Children are one of the ultimate blessings we can have. This is why abortion is one of the ultimate forms of the depravity of mankind. Even the beasts will gladly sacrifice their own lives for the sake of their offspring. Only the lowest forms of life, or the most cruel, would ever kill their own young.

The very first test of Solomon's wisdom was to distinguish the careless mother from the one who esteemed the life of her child. This is still the basis of true wisdom. Careless means to care-less. Careful means to be full-of-caring. Love is full of caring for others. God is love, and if we are to be restored to the image of God, we must love, which is to be full of caring.

Fundamental to nature is to care for the young. However, because of the fall, the nature we were created with has been severely perverted. True Christianity is a restoration from the place from which we have fallen. This is why it is written in I Timothy 5:8, **"But if anyone does not provide for his own, and especially for those of his household, he has denied the faith, and is worse than an unbeliever."** If we do not care for the little ones who have been entrusted to us, we are denying that redemption, which is the redemption of our fallen nature.

In John 15:1-8 the Lord makes a clear declaration concerning bearing fruit:

I am the true vine, and My Father is the vinedresser.
Every branch in Me that does not bear fruit, He takes away; and every branch that bears fruit, He prunes it, that it may bear more fruit.

You are already clean because of the word which I have spoken to you.

Abide in Me, and I in you. As the branch cannot bear fruit of itself, unless it abides in the vine, so neither can you, unless you abide in Me.

I am the vine, you are the branches; he who abides in Me, and I in him, he bears much fruit; for apart from Me you can do nothing.

If anyone does not abide in Me, he is thrown away as a branch, and dries up; and they gather them, and cast them into the fire, and they are burned.

If you abide in Me, and My words abide in you, ask whatever you wish, and it shall be done for you.

By this is My Father glorified, that you bear much fruit, and so prove to be My disciples.

If we have true spiritual life, we will bear fruit and multiply spiritually. Galatians 5:22-23 says, **"But the fruit of the Spirit is love, joy, peace, patience, kindness, goodness, faithfulness, gentleness, self-control..."** If we are abiding in the Lord, we should be growing in each of these aspects of the fruit of the Spirit. If we are not growing in fruit, we are obviously not abiding in the Lord.

True Christianity is "the path of life." Jesus came to give life, and to give it abundantly (see John 10:10). It is fundamental to our faith to esteem life. In contrast, the devil was **"a murderer from the beginning" (John 8:44).** Those who walk the path of life will not only esteem and protect life, but they will multiply life just as God's first blessing to man made possible. If we are walking as we should, we will be leaving behind a trail of life and fruitfulness. The Blessed Creator loves life. He wants to see the world swarming with it. Those who abide in Him will be fruitful, reproducing, and loving life.

DAY 13

Diversity

Then God said, "Let the earth bring forth living creatures after their kind: cattle and creeping things and beasts of the earth after their kind;" and it was so.

And God made the beasts of the earth after their kind, and the cattle after their kind, and everything that creeps on the ground after its kind; and God saw that it was good (Genesis 1:24-25).

God created every species to reproduce **"after their kind."** It is noteworthy that a fundamental aspect of the theory of evolution is that species evolved, but to date there is not a single record of one species being able to mate with another species and bring forth offspring that can reproduce. You can mate a horse with a donkey and bring forth mules, but mules cannot reproduce. This is a law that God set in the genetic code of His creation in order to preserve the uniqueness of each creature.

The Lord so loves diversity that He made every snowflake different. He made every tree and person different. His creativity continues to expand with every new plant or creature that is brought forth. Even when Jesus walked the earth, He never healed people the same way twice. In every new setting He had a different message. There is a newness and freshness to God every day. Walking with Him is to be in a continual state of awe and marvel. Yet, the foundation of this exploding creativity is set within boundaries that allow it to flow in a beautiful and orderly symmetry, not chaos.

This also brings up an interesting question about whether God intended for there to be a mingling of the human races. It is important that the special gifts and characteristics which God imparted to races and cultures be preserved, so that they can make their contribution to the revelation of God. He made man in His image for the purpose of revealing Himself to the natural creation, and it takes the combined gifts of all races and cultures for God to fully reveal Himself. However, the boundary that was to be protected in order for all to reproduce

"after their kind" was the boundary of species, not races. Since races can join and their offspring continue to reproduce, this indicates that it does not violate the Lord's original purpose. The mingling of races brings forth new revelations of His creativity within the bounds He has set.

As stated, those who are becoming like the Lord will obviously love creativity. Those who know the blessed Creator, and are becoming like Him, should be creative. We should love diversity, and yet respect order and purpose. When properly combined, we will be much closer to becoming like Him.

If we have His heart for diversity and creativity, whenever we meet someone who is different from us, we will be open and expectant of learning something, not closed and fearful. One of the distinguishing characteristics between the "sheep and goats" is when the Lord came to them as a stranger, and the sheep took Him in (see Matthew 25:32-36). The Greek word translated "stranger" is *xenos* (xen'-os), which is literally a "foreigner or alien." The Lord often comes to us through those who are different from us. If we are not open to them, we will not be open to Him either.

In Mark 16, we have the story of the two men on the road to Emmaus who could not recognize the Lord because it says that **"He appeared in a different form to two of them" (Mark 16:12).** He obviously did this purposely so that they would recognize Him after the Spirit, and not just appearance. It is also likely that the main reason why we often fail to recognize Him when He tries to draw near to us is that He often comes to us in forms that we are not used to. If we are a Baptist, He may come to us as a Pentecostal. If we are a Charismatic, He may come to us as a Baptist, etc. He is continually trying to break down the barriers of our religious racism.

Racism is born from the two great evils of pride and fear. It is an ultimate form of pride when we believe we are better than others because of our race. Religious racism is the belief that we are better than others because we are a part of a certain denomination or movement. As James 4:6 declares, **"God is opposed to the proud, but gives grace to the humble."** Such pride can be one of the most destructive forces in our lives. It will also turn us into one of those that the Lord referred to as "goats," because we will refuse to open our hearts to those who are different from us. Racism can be rooted in either pride or fear, but both are evil, and both are contrary to the love of God that is the foundation of all truth.

DAY 14

The Crown

Then God said, "Let Us make man in Our image, according to Our likeness (Genesis 1:26).

What greater honor could there possibly be than to be created in the image of God? Man is the crown of God's creation. Man is the one to most reflect His nature; this is the ultimate purpose of man. If there is any way for us to measure the success of our lives, it would be by how well we have reflected Him in our lives. For this reason we read in Romans 8:28-30:

And we know that God causes all things to work together for good to those who love God, to those who are called according to His purpose.

For whom He foreknew, He also predestined to become conformed to the image of His Son, that He might be the first-born among many brethren;

and whom He predestined, these He also called; and whom He called, these He also justified; and whom He justified, these He also glorified.

The fall of man did not disrupt God's ultimate calling upon men, but only delayed it a little. The Lord used the fall to reveal His unfathomable love, and to bring forth a "new creation" that was much higher than the first creation. Those who overcome the fall by their faith in the cross of Jesus Christ, will become joint heirs with Him.

For this reason **"God causes all things to work together for good to those who love God, to those who are called according to His purpose" (Romans 8:28).** Everything that happens to us is for the purpose of bringing forth God's higher purpose in our lives. That higher purpose is Christlikeness. Every trial and every problem is for the purpose of conforming us to the image of Christ. If we will look at our problems in that light, we will be able to understand and overcome them. In all things we must keep the high calling of being conformed to the image of Christ as our purpose.

To understand our transformation we must understand II Corinthians 3:18: **"But we all, with unveiled face beholding as in a mirror the glory of the Lord, are being transformed into the same image from glory to glory, just as from the Lord, the Spirit."** We are to be transformed **"from glory to glory."** This indicates an unfolding process to change us into His image. This is not a process that we can engineer or control, but it is **"from the Lord, the Spirit."** All that we can do is to submit to it. We submit to it by **"beholding the glory of the Lord."** As we behold His glory, we will be changed into His image.

When we fall into the trap of trying to change ourselves, it results in looking at ourselves instead of Him. This will inevitably lead to the black hole of self-centeredness. Even after we are born again into the Lord, transformation needs to take place in our lives. However, we will never be changed by dwelling on what is wrong with us, but rather by beholding the glory of the Lord. As we keep our attention on Him, we will change, even if we are often unaware of it.

John the Baptist said, **"He must increase, but I must decrease" (John 3:30).** Many, seeking to emulate this noble devotion, have determined they must decrease so that He can increase, but that is not what John said. It is in fact the opposite and will bring about the very opposite results we are seeking which is to be like Christ. If we are trying to decrease so He can increase, it is still we who are in control. For us to be transformed into His image, **"He must increase,"** and then we will decrease. If we get this backwards, it will result in the religious spirit of the Pharisees.

He increases in us as we behold His glory, not our own shortcomings. The Holy Spirit was sent to convict us of sin, and He will point out our sin. The remedy is to repent. Repentance is not just turning away from the sin, but it is turning to the Lord. If we only take a half step of turning from the sin, we will fall again. We must turn to the Lord, fleeing to the power of His cross, beholding His glory and nature. Then we will be changed. Therefore, when we sin, we must not run from the Lord, but rather to Him.

> **For we do not have a high priest who cannot sympathize with our weaknesses, but one who has been tempted in all things as we are, yet without sin.**
> **Let us therefore draw near with confidence to the throne of grace, that we may receive mercy and may find grace to help in time of need (Hebrews 4:15-16).**

DAY 15

Authority

"and let them rule over the fish of the sea and over the birds of the sky and over the cattle and over all the earth, and over every creeping thing that creeps on the earth" **(Genesis 1:26).**

The Lord is the King of Kings and Lord of Lords. It is, therefore, a part of the image of God for man to rule over **"all the earth."** However, because most of mankind has listened to the devil more than to God for so long, the things that we still have the power to do, such as rule over the earth, we often do more like the devil than like God. Evil authority thinks that all they rule over exists for them. Godlike authority exists for the sake of those over which they rule. Godly authority is not a privilege, but a responsibility.

Romans 6:16 explains a basic principle of authority: **"Do you not know that when you present yourselves to someone as slaves for obedience, you are slaves of the one whom you obey, either of sin resulting in death, or of obedience resulting in righteousness?"** It is a principle that we become slaves to the one whom we obey. When Adam obeyed Satan by eating the forbidden fruit, he became a slave to Satan along with the domain that had been entrusted to him. The result is declared in I John 5:19: **"and the whole world lies in the power of the evil one."**

When the image of God was marred in man by the fall, the definition of our purpose was also twisted. As we are redeemed and begin to recover the image of God, we will also recover the proper exercise of authority. Our nature is to **"rule,"** but if we rule before we have been restored in the image of God, it will be a perversion of authority. If we seek to be like Him more than we seek authority, we can be trusted with more authority. Only as we keep Christlikeness as our primary goal, will we stay on the path to recovering His rule over the earth, which is the coming of His kingdom. As we do this, we will exercise authority as He does, for the sake of and service to those who are ruled over, as we read in Matthew 20:25-28:

But Jesus called them to Himself, and said, "You know that the rulers of the Gentiles lord it over them, and their great men exercise authority over them.

"It is not so among you, but whoever wishes to become great among you shall be your servant,

and whoever wishes to be first among you shall be your slave;

just as the Son of Man did not come to be served, but to serve, and to give His life a ransom for many."

Jesus is the **"last Adam" (I Corinthians 15:45).** He had to become a man to recover what was lost by man. As we see the theme repeated throughout the New Testament, Jesus did not come just to redeem man, but to redeem the world, or everything that was under Adam's domain. The kingdom of God is the place where the authority of Jesus is recognized. Our calling is to proclaim the message of the kingdom, that the earth has been redeemed. When the message has been fully proclaimed, the King will come and take the authority that He purchased with His own life. However, we can only be ambassadors for the kingdom if we are citizens of the kingdom ourselves. We must live under the authority of Jesus now, if we are to proclaim His kingdom.

We read in Matthew 8:8-10 the story of the centurion with great faith. We see that understanding authority is also basic to walking in faith:

But the centurion answered and said, "Lord, I am not worthy for You to come under my roof, but just say the word, and my servant will be healed.

"For I, too, am a man under authority, with soldiers under me; and I say to this one, 'Go!' and he goes, and to another, 'Come!' and he comes, and to my slave, 'Do this!' and he does it."

Now when Jesus heard this, He marveled, and said to those who were following, "Truly I say to you, I have not found such great faith with anyone in Israel."

Faith is the basis of authority for miracles. We will only have true authority to the degree that we are under the authority of the King. True faith is the result of being obedient to Him. When we are fully under His authority, He will then be able to trust us with full authority.

DAY 16

Unity

And God created man in His own image, in the image of God He created him; male and female He created them (Genesis 1:27).

Man was originally created male and female. After the woman was taken from man, it would take both the man and the woman, in unity, to reveal the image of God. No man can fully reveal the image of God, and neither can any woman. We need each other, and this is why one of the primary assaults of the devil is to deceive men and women into thinking that they do not need each other. Therefore, homosexuality is one of the ultimate perversions of the purpose for which we were created.

For this reason, if the devil cannot push men and women into homosexuality, he will at least try to blur the distinctions between them. He will try to get men to become like women, and women like men, so that true unity can never be achieved by them. The way a man becomes one with his wife is not by making her into man, but rather by acknowledging, and honoring her differences. Likewise, the only way that a woman can become one with her husband is by acknowledging and honoring the ways that he is different.

In general, women have strengths and perspectives that men do not have, and men have strengths and perspectives that women do not have. This is not stereotyping; it is simply acknowledging a fact that one has to be both spiritually and scientifically blind not to see. The way we become one, so that we can reflect the image of God, is by acknowledging our differences, and seeing them as complimentary, not contradictory.

II Corinthians 3:18 states, **"But we all, with unveiled face beholding as in a mirror the glory of the Lord, are being transformed into the same image from glory to glory, just as from the Lord, the Spirit."** To be transformed into the image of the Lord, requires that we see His glory *with an unveiled face*. There are many veils the devil seeks to place on mankind, so that even if we see the Lord's glory, we will distort it, and pervert the true reflection of Him. Though the image of the Lord is both male and female, and there is the nature of Him that would gather us as a hen gathers her chicks, God is presented throughout the Scriptures as "Father," and is never called "Mother." To dilute this, is to distort His image with a very thick veil.

"Father" means "life giver." The father gives the seed, and the mother nurtures the seed. In Scripture, we see the creation as "a" mother. Both Israel and the church are also referred to in Scripture as "mothers." Just as the woman was taken from Adam so that they would have to come together to be the complete image of God, the Lord will be joined perfectly to His bride to give the creation a true reflection of His glory. However, there can be no joining if we do not see the differences of each. God is the Father, and He is masculine to the uttermost. We must not compromise this basic truth if we are to see His glory and be changed into His image.

The roles of men and women are being severely challenged in our times. However, that which the enemy intends for evil always turns out for the good of those who love God. The church is also struggling with understanding the roles God intended for men and women. We must use this challenge to search even more diligently for God's answer to these questions. When men become the men they are called to be, and women become the women they are called to be, the whole world will stand in awe of them, knowing in the depths of their hearts that they reflect who they are called to be.

The apostle Paul stated in I Corinthians 4:15: **"For if you were to have countless tutors in Christ, yet you would not have many fathers."** The same is true of the church today. There are many teachers, but not many fathers who are reproducing. That is why most great churches and movements tend to die with the death of their founders. They did not reproduce their ministry in others or it would carry on and multiply. One reason there are not many true spiritual fathers in the church, is for one to become a father, a woman must be present. Until women are able to take their rightful place in the church, there will continue to be limited reproduction. This is a crucial issue for our times. It is obvious that the world will continue to fall into a deeper depravity concerning women's liberation if the church does not seize and promote the true liberation of women. No one desires to liberate women more than the Lord. Neither will men be truly liberated until women are. If any part of the body of Christ is still in bondage, we all are.

DAY 17

The Commission

> And God blessed them; and God said to them, "Be fruitful and multiply, and fill the earth, and subdue it; and rule over the fish of the sea and over the birds of the sky, and over every living thing that moves on the earth."
>
> Then God said, "Behold, I have given you every plant yielding seed that is on the surface of all the earth, and every tree which has fruit yielding seed; it shall be food for you;
>
> and to every beast of the earth and to every bird of the sky and to every thing that moves on the earth which has life, I have given every green plant for food"; and it was so.
>
> And God saw all that He had made, and behold, it was very good. And there was evening and there was morning, the sixth day (Genesis 1:28-31).

Again, the Lord blessed His creation, and told them to be fruitful, to fill the earth, subdue it, and rule over it. The blessing of the Lord is sure, and even after the disobedience of man, the blessing was still upon him to accomplish all of these things. He has been fruitful and multiplied, filling the earth, subduing it, and ruling over it. God created man for this, so it is not wrong. Some have a belief that whatever man does is not natural, but man is a part of nature too. The earth cannot be what it was created to be without man filling it, subduing it, and ruling over it, just as the Lord originally planned.

However, because of the perversion of man's nature by sin, and the cruelty of death that was released by sin, the way in which man has subdued the earth and ruled over it has been tragically distorted by his selfishness. As stated, the rulership that the Lord originally created was not for dominance, but for service. Man was to rule over the creation for the sake of the creation. When man is redeemed and restored, the integrity of this rulership will also be restored.

When "the last Adam," Jesus, returns to set up His kingdom, it will be a restoration of the original commission to the first Adam. Here Isaiah prophesied concerning the coming of His kingdom:

> **And the wolf will dwell with the lamb, and the leopard will lie down with the kid, and the calf and the young lion and the fatling together; and a little boy will lead them.**
>
> **Also the cow and the bear will graze; their young will lie down together; and the lion will eat straw like the ox.**
>
> **And the nursing child will play by the hole of the cobra, and the weaned child will put his hand on the viper's den.**
>
> **They will not hurt or destroy in all My holy mountain, for the earth will be full of the knowledge of the LORD as the waters cover the sea (Isaiah 11:6-9).**

This is a greater hope than even the most optimistic philosophers have been able to imagine in their utopias. This is the sure hope that we have in Christ, and it is a hope that will not disappoint. As Peter declared, there will be a **"restoration of all things,"** so let us:

> **"Repent therefore and return, that your sins may be wiped away, in order that times of refreshing may come from the presence of the Lord;**
>
> **and that He may send Jesus, the Christ appointed for you,**
>
> **whom heaven must receive until the period of restoration of all things about which God spoke by the mouth of His holy prophets from ancient time (Acts 3:19-21).**

The more we return to Jesus, and the closer we get to Him, the more we will become righteous in our reigning. When men are restored to reigning in righteousness, the order and harmony of the whole creation will be restored. The whole earth will become like the original Garden of Eden. There will be no more hunger, wars, child abuse, sickness, or death. The work that Jesus did on the cross was for the **"restoration of all things."** Through the saga of man's history all of creation will have learned not only the consequences of sin, but also the expanse of God's love and forgiveness.

If all of this was accomplished by Jesus on the cross, why didn't He immediately bind Satan, cast him into the lake of fire, and begin this restoration immediately upon His resurrection? Because it was also a part of His primary purpose to have a bride, a queen to reign with Him over the age to come. This queen had to prove herself worthy of such great authority before the angels and principalities and powers in the heavenly places. The bride of the first Adam lived in a perfect world, and yet chose to sin. The bride of the Last Adam will live in the most wicked of times, but choose to be obedient against even the greatest opposition. Therefore, all of creation will know that she, the church, is worthy to reign with the Lamb.

DAY 18

The Sabbath

Thus the heavens and the earth were completed, and all their hosts.

And by the seventh day God completed His work which He had done; and He rested on the seventh day from all His work which He had done.

Then God blessed the seventh day and sanctified it, because in it He rested from all His work which God had created and made.

This is the account of the heavens and the earth when they were created, in the day that the LORD God made earth and heaven (Genesis 2:1-4).

Because man was created at the end of the sixth day, his first full day was the seventh day of creation, the day God rested. For man to have fellowship with God from the beginning, he had to start by entering God's rest, and this is still essential for true fellowship with God. This is why the Promised Land is equated with the rest of God in Hebrews 3-4. He created man to need rest. However, the rest he needs is more than just sleeping.

In Psalm 46:10 the Lord says, **"Cease striving and know that I am God."** Striving is a demonstration of the fact that we really do not know God as He is. If we know Him as He is, we know that He is above all authority, power, and dominion. If we know Him as He is, we can trust that He is in control, and that He really will work all things together for our good. This brings rest, peace, and security that is incomprehensible to those who do not know the Lord. Peace and rest in the midst of any situation should be the hallmarks of every believer.

Striving is the result of worry, and worry is the result of not having faith in God. This is sin, as we read in Romans 14:23, **"whatever is not from faith is sin."** In I Peter 5:6-7 we are exhorted to, **"Humble yourselves, therefore, under the mighty hand of God, that He may exalt you at the proper time, casting all your anxiety upon Him,**

because He cares for you." The way we humble ourselves before God is to cast our anxiety upon Him. Anxiety is pride. It is pride to think that any problem is too big for God, and we have to straighten it out ourselves!

It took faith to enter the Promised Land. Doubt caused an entire generation to perish in the wilderness. Many Christians, likewise, do not attain to the promises of God in their lives, because they allow doubt to control them instead of faith. One of the primary ways we demonstrate faith is to rest in His promises, and in who He is. If we really trust Him, we will have rest and peace, even in the midst of our trials.

In Ezekiel 44:18 we are told concerning the priests, **"Linen turbans shall be on their heads, and linen undergarments shall be on their loins; they shall not gird themselves with anything which makes them sweat."** Sweat is the result of exerting our own strength, so sweat speaks of a ministry that comes from our own efforts. If we are going to be the priests of the Lord, we must not take on anything that makes us sweat. The Lord beckons us in Matthew 11:28-30:

> **"Come to Me, all who are weary and heavy-laden, and I will give you rest.**
> **"Take My yoke upon you, and learn from Me, for I am gentle and humble in heart; and you shall find rest for your souls.**
> **"For My yoke is easy, and My load is light."**

A yoke speaks of work, but when we are yoked with the Lord, it will be His strength that does the work, and we just get carried along for the ride! It is the Spirit that He has given to us that will do the work, just as He did from the beginning. We are told in Acts 7:48, **"the Most High does not dwell in houses made by human hands."** Paul the apostle explained to the men of Athens in Acts 17:25, **"neither is He served by human hands, as though He needed anything."** All of our best efforts will not accomplish anything for Him. We are simply called to obedience and abiding in Him. When we come to rest in Him, He will then move through us, and we will actually find rest and refreshment as He does it.

We see in His call that we need to be yoked with Him. By doing this, we learn from Him to be gentle and humble. When we depart from these two great qualities of the Lord, we will begin to work in our own strength. We know that when we begin to sweat and strive, we have departed from abiding in Him, and from the rest that we have in Him. When we abide in His rest, we are always refreshed instead of drained.

DAY 19

God and Man

Now no shrub of the field was yet in the earth, and no plant of the field had yet sprouted, for the LORD God had not sent rain upon the earth; and there was no man to cultivate the ground.

But a mist used to rise from the earth and water the whole surface of the ground.

Then the LORD God formed man of dust from the ground, and breathed into his nostrils the breath of life; and man became a living being (Genesis 2:5-7).

Why didn't the Lord just speak man into being, like He did other parts of the creation? Instead He formed man, and fashioned him like an artist with his pottery. He then breathed His own life into man. The word that is translated **"breath"** in this text is the Hebrew word *neshamah* (nesh-aw-maw'), which could have been translated "divine inspiration," or "intellect." Man was to be made in the image of God, not just in appearance, but with some of His own ability to reason and perceive. Man was to be unique in the creation.

Man was fashioned from the earth, and the earth was to be his realm, but he was also born with a heart to reach for the God who created Him. God is Spirit, and man was created to have a special fellowship with God who is Spirit. Because of this, there is a spiritual void in every human being that can only be truly fulfilled when in fellowship with God.

Man is natural, and born from the earth, but he was given his spark of life from God who is supernatural. Because of this, there is a yearning for the supernatural in man. If this spiritual hunger, and attraction for the supernatural, is not filled with a relationship to God, man has proven repeatedly that he will fill the void with the most base forms of spiritism and the demonic supernatural. As the saying goes, "If you deny a man food he will gobble poison." Man must have God.

Without God, our most noble ventures, and our highest successes, will still leave us empty. We were created for Him, and the very breath that we breathe yearns for the One who gave it to us. We were created for Him, and we will never be complete without Him. The entire six thousand-year history of man declares this truth with bold underlines. We have tried to substitute everything for God, but now we know that it is better to lose everything than to lose our relationship with Him.

To have fellowship with God is essential and elementary to our being, but it is also an unfathomable privilege. What could possibly be more exciting than to have fellowship with the Almighty? What could possibly be more interesting? As King David asked, why would the Lord even be interested in man? It is hard to understand, but God loves us, and wants to be close to us. We were created for God's pleasure! The One who stretched out the heavens like a tent curtain enjoys being close to man. Is it not our greatest and most tragic folly to fail to take advantage of this incomprehensible opportunity to have fellowship with Him?

In I Corinthians 1:6-9, the apostle Paul states all of this with extraordinary brevity and clarity:

> **even as the testimony concerning Christ was confirmed in you,**
> **so that you are not lacking in any gift, awaiting eagerly the revelation of our Lord Jesus Christ,**
> **who shall also confirm you to the end, blameless in the day of our Lord Jesus Christ.**
> **God is faithful, through whom you were called into fellowship with His Son, Jesus Christ our Lord.**

The testimony concerning Christ is confirmed in us when we are not lacking in any gift. The gifts of the Spirit are named in I Corinthians 12:4-12, and we are told in verse 31 to **"earnestly desire the greater gifts,"** and again in I Corinthians 14:1 to **"Pursue love, yet desire earnestly spiritual gifts, but especially that you may prophesy."** Jesus demonstrated all of the gifts of the Spirit in His ministry. Therefore, the testimony that Christ is fully functioning through us is confirmed when all of the gifts are functioning through us. This is not singular, but corporate. He has distributed the gifts to individuals so that we must come together for the full testimony of Him to be confirmed through us.

It is right for us to "earnestly desire" spiritual gifts. This fulfills the yearning for the supernatural that is in every human soul because we were created to have fellowship with a supernatural God. Through the moving of the Spirit that is given to us, we have fellowship with Christ. When the Spirit moves through us to heal, we are touched by His compassion for the sick. When He speaks a prophetic word through us, we are touched by what is on His heart, etc. Having spiritual gifts is a way we have fellowship with God who is Spirit.

DAY 20

Labor

And the LORD God planted a garden toward the east, in Eden; and there He placed the man whom He had formed.

And out of the ground the LORD God caused to grow every tree that is pleasing to the sight and good for food; the tree of life also in the midst of the garden, and the tree of the knowledge of good and evil.

Then the LORD God took the man and put him into the garden of Eden to cultivate it and keep it (Genesis 2:8,9,15).

The Lord carefully and wonderfully prepared a perfect environment for man. He created man and He knew exactly what would be best for him, and what he would enjoy. He also created man to cultivate his own environment, and this required labor. Some have mistakenly believed that labor was a part of the curse, but man labored in the Garden before the fall. Labor was not a part of the curse; "toil" was the curse. Toil is different from labor. To toil is to accomplish only with hard and painful labor. Toil implies the opposition of the creation instead of its cooperation.

Man was created for fellowship with God, and for cultivating the earth. Therefore, man was also created to labor, and meaningful labor is essential for the well-being and fulfillment of man. The key word here is "meaningful." The Lord intended for us to receive a deep satisfaction from our labors. Without meaningful accomplishment in our lives, there will be another void that leaves us empty and disoriented. It is also fundamental that every person find meaningful labor.

There are two Hebrew words translated into the one English word "cultivate" in this chapter. They are `bad (aw-bad'), which means "to serve, till," etc. The other is *shaman* (shaw-mar'), which means to "hedge about, guard, protect," etc. These are both inherent characteristics of man. We read previously in Genesis 2:5, **"Now no shrub of the field was yet in the earth, and no plant of the field had yet sprouted, for the LORD God had not sent rain upon the earth; and there was no man to cultivate the ground."** The Lord had even left part of His planned creation for man to help bring forth.

It is a part of our very nature to take what the Lord has provided for us, and add our own touch to it. This may even seem sacrilegious to some, but not when we understand that the Lord left this for man to do so that man could express the creative nature that He had put in him. God wanted man's touch in the garden. He wanted man to also "own it" in his heart so that he would be compelled to keep and protect it. Of course, this was to be done with God, but the Lord wanted man to contribute.

Our nature is to look for ways to add our own touch to things, to improve them, and to be protective of domains with which we are entrusted. As with all of our gifts and characteristics, if they are not used rightly, they will be used wrongly. If they are not used constructively, they will be used destructively. Even so, man was created to be creative, which is a basic part of the image of God that we have been given.

Man is called to rest in God, but we must also labor with God. In this labor, we must find what He created us to do. We are told in Ephesians 1:4 that, **He chose us in Him before the foundation of the world, that we should be holy and blameless before Him. In love.** We were foreknown and chosen by God before the world was even created. The God who is so particular and specific also knew what He created us for. We each have a very specific job to do—a very specific calling. We will never know a true peace and fulfillment in our hearts until we are doing our callings.

How do we know what our calling is? This may be to oversimplify it a little, but we find out in the last two words of Ephesians 1:4 **In love.** Because we were created with our purpose in mind, what we are called to do will also be what we love to do the most. We are told in John 7:38, **"He who believes in Me, as the Scripture said, 'From his innermost being shall flow rivers of living water.'"** Living waters can only come from our hearts, that which is our deepest love.

God has created us and called us to do the deepest desire of our heart. However, most people are so burdened and bound by other people's expectations and yokes that it takes complete "renewing" of their minds before they begin to discern the yoke that God has called them to carry. Even so, we must pursue this quest and not give up until we are living in peace and fulfillment which can only come when we know we are doing what we were created to do.

DAY 21

The Test

And the LORD God commanded the man, saying, "From any tree of the garden you may eat freely;
but from the tree of the knowledge of good and evil you shall not eat, for in the day that you eat from it you shall surely die" (Genesis 2:16-17).

The Lord did not place the forbidden tree in the garden in order to cause man to fall. He put it there to give them a place to prove their obedience and commitment to Him. There can be no true obedience from the heart if there is not the freedom to disobey. The Lord established that man would have to make choices. We have been created to have fellowship with God, and for productive labor. Man was also created to be free, and we will never be fulfilled until we are free.

Freedom is the natural state of man. Freedom is also difficult. We cannot have freedom without taking the responsibility that comes with it. The freedom that God gave to man to reach for extraordinary accomplishments can also lead to tragic mistakes. Mistakes have consequences. Even so, we cannot escape our calling to freedom. It may be easier to live with someone else making all of the important decisions for us, but without freedom we will be perpetually frustrated and stifled in a profound way because we were created to be free.

Some of the most fulfilling experiences in life come when we take initiative, make a good choice, and see the fruit. The most discouraging and hurtful experiences come when we choose to do wrong. To avoid the latter, many choose a life of bondage in cults or authoritarian groups who make all of the decisions for their people. However, as the German people learned in World War II, this always leads to even worse consequences. We were created to have freedom, and we can never become who we were created to be without it. Let us accept the great responsibility that comes with freedom, and choose rightly.

Many also fall into the bondage of trying to live under the law to escape the responsibility of being free. We tend to think of the Old

Testament as the law and the New Testament as grace, but that is not necessarily true. The Old Covenant is the letter, and the New Covenant is in the Spirit. If the New Covenant is read without the Spirit, it will just be law. Therefore, righteousness will attempt to be established by complying with the letter, instead of seeking to abide in Christ.

The Old and New Testaments are the written Word of God to us. As Jesus said, **"the Scripture cannot be broken" (John 10:35),** meaning that they are a single unity. In fact, everywhere in the New Testament, "the Scriptures" referred to are in relation to the Old Testament books, as the New Testament was just then being written. The Old Testament is the foundation for New Testament faith. The Old Testament Scriptures were the basis for doctrines upon which the church is based, as well as the gospel of the kingdom (see Romans 16:25-26; Acts 28:23). Of course, it was also the books we call the Old Testament that Jesus used and referred to in all of His messages, as we see in Luke 24:25-27:

> **And He said to them, "O foolish men and slow of heart to believe in all that the prophets have spoken!**
> **"Was it not necessary for the Christ to suffer these things and to enter into His glory?"**
> **And beginning with Moses and with all the prophets, He explained to them the things concerning Himself in all the Scriptures.**

In John 5:46-47 He makes an important statement about this:

> **"For if you believed Moses, you would believe Me; for he wrote of Me.**
> **"But if you do not believe his writings, how will you believe My words?"**

If the One who is the Word Himself used the Scriptures as the basis for all of His teachings, how much more do we need to be devoted to them? Even so, if in seeking to be a biblical people, we forbid anyone to do that which is not specifically written in the New Testament, we have only turned it into another law. It was not meant to bind us in that way, but to free us to do whatever is not specifically forbidden by it. This does not make everything that is not specifically forbidden by it right, but it casts upon us the responsibility to know the Lord's voice and follow the Holy Spirit. This is a great responsibility, but without it there could not be a true relationship with Him. Without this freedom, we would still be married to the law. As

Paul explained in Galatians 5:4, **"You have been severed from Christ, you who are seeking to be justified by law; you have fallen from grace."** Therefore, **"It was for freedom that Christ set us free; therefore keep standing firm and do not be subject again to a yoke of slavery" (Galatians 5:1).**

DAY 22

Fellowship

> **Then the LORD God said, "It is not good for the man to be alone; I will make him a helper suitable for him."**
>
> **And out of the ground the LORD God formed every beast of the field and every bird of the sky, and brought them to the man to see what he would call them; and whatever the man called a living creature, that was its name.**
>
> **And the man gave names to all the cattle, and to the birds of the sky, and to every beast of the field, but for Adam there was not found a helper suitable for him (Genesis 2:18-20).**

Man was created to be a social creature. God said, **"it is not good for man to be alone."** It is interesting that man was lonely even though he had fellowship with God. This implies that God alone was not enough for man. This may be a shocking thought, but the Lord created man to need fellowship with Him, as well as with those of his own kind.

The Lord allowed the man to seek through all of creation to find the helper suitable for him, but one was not found. The Lord knows the end from the beginning, so why didn't He just tell the man that none of these helpers was the one that he was seeking, and put him to sleep and bring forth the woman? It is for the same reason that the Lord will often let us chase many endeavors in our lives to seek fulfillment, even though He already knows this is futile. The Lord created man to be free and He will not violate that freedom. The Lord had already said that He would make a helper suitable to man, but man still had to search, and the Lord let him. He will also let us chase many fruitless endeavors, if we insist on having to prove something to ourselves.

Many still spend their lives making the same search that Adam did. They can view women as sex objects, but not as the source of fellowship that can touch the deepest needs of their heart, and cure the loneliness. Therefore, men often seek fulfillment in their professions, sports, hobbies, raising animals, etc. These are not necessarily bad, and can be fulfilling to a degree, but none of these will ever be suitable for filling the void that can only be filled when the suitable helpmate is found.

However, we must not esteem the fellowship with our mates above our fellowship with God. Our need for Him is greater. Nevertheless, there will be a void in our hearts that can only be filled with a proper relationship to our mates. We must have fellowship with God and our mates to be complete. The proper relationship between a man and a woman is a wonderful relationship that God created to help us better understand our union with Him. This relationship is needed, but it can never substitute for the greater need for Him.

If we do not love God more than we love our mates, we will not love our mates as much as we should. Our relationship to God was created first and must always remain first. Even so, as we see in I John 4:20: **If someone says, "I love God," and hates his brother, he is a liar; for the one who does not love his brother whom he has seen, cannot love God whom he has not seen.** Our relationship to other people is a good barometer of our relationship to God. If we truly love God, it will be manifested in our love for others. This will be especially true in our love for our mates, which is intended to be a reflection of Christ's love for the church.

Because loneliness is the first thing God said was not good, if we are seeking to love and help our neighbors, we should especially watch out for the lonely. This does not just mean those who are living alone. You can be in a crowd and be lonely. Loneliness is the result of not having fellowship that goes beyond the superficial to touch the soul. Deep, meaningful fellowship is essential for our mental, physical, and spiritual wholeness. The fellowship that we were created to have is not an either/or situation between God and men, but rather both. If we are lonely, it is because we have not kept the balance between them properly.

Even so, many try to find the fulfillment that they can only find in their relationship to God through their mates, or others, and even those in the church. Usually, this will lead to frustration that will damage our relationship to our mates and others, because we will begin to feel that they are not enough for us. They aren't, because they can never take the place of God in our lives.

DAY 23

Marriage

So the LORD God caused a deep sleep to fall upon the man, and he slept; then He took one of his ribs, and closed up the flesh at that place.

And the LORD God fashioned into a woman the rib which He had taken from the man, and brought her to the man.

And the man said, "This is now bone of my bones, and flesh of my flesh; she shall be called Woman, because she was taken out of Man" (Genesis 2:21-23).

God's remedy for the one thing about His creation that was not good was to make a helper that was **"suitable"** to man. The Hebrew word that is translated **"suitable"** here is *neged* (neh'-ghed), which could have been translated "opposite part" or a "counterpart." To be a helpmate, the woman needed to be different from the man—not a difference that conflicted with him, but rather one that complimented him. She would have the part that he was missing. To be whole he needed her, and she needed him. It has been a primary strategy of the enemy to blur the distinctions between men and women and deceive them into thinking they do not need each other.

As soon as the man saw the woman, his heart leapt and he knew she was the one! The man looked at the woman and was charged, but it did not appear to have done the same for Eve. Men tend to be stimulated more by sight than women. Just looking at Eve was enough to convince Adam, but just looking at Adam probably did not do much for Eve. However, the words that Adam spoke probably did mean something to her.

God created romance and sex, and both are to be a wonderful and intimate expression of love between a man and woman. However, He created mankind to be body, soul, and spirit. Romance was created to be more than sex. It was to be a union of spirit, soul, and body, in that order. If the order is reversed so that the union of bodies is esteemed first, then it is unlikely that the union of spirit and soul will take place, and the loneliness will continue.

This is why the Lord created the institution of marriage, and sanctioned that sex outside of marriage is a sin against Him. It is a sin against the very nature of man that God created. Mankind was created to be creatures of lofty intelligence and spirituality. They were also physical creatures who were "wonderfully made." The Lord wanted the crown of His creation to be whole and fulfilled on all three levels, and if mankind started esteeming the physical above the others, a basic perversion of their nature would occur. Therefore, sex was to be an expression of the love and union of spirit and soul. Only as it was this expression of love and union, would it truly be fulfilling, and remain the high and lofty expression that it was intended to be. There is a spiritual sensuality that can be released through the love and union of spirit and soul that physical sensuality can never compare with.

In the first meeting of Adam and Eve, Adam was immediately convinced that they were right for each other. It appears that Eve may have taken a little more convincing. She was different, and probably needed to be touched more in her soul and spirit before she could be fully convinced. God made women this way to call men to higher levels of experience. Women do tend to be more spiritually oriented, and often interpreted as more emotional, because they tend to be more in touch with their spiritual senses.

Since the fall, women have been blamed because Eve was deceived and offered the forbidden fruit to Adam. However, this implies that Adam was not deceived, and sinned even though he knew what he was doing. That is far more sinister. Why did Adam follow Eve that way? It was probably because she had been created to help call Adam to the higher realms of spirituality, and Adam had already learned to follow her in this. It is basic to the devil's strategy to turn our strengths into weaknesses, and use them against us. He seldom tries to stop someone from doing what they are called to do. He learned in the beginning that it is far more effective to get behind them and push them too far.

We will examine these issues in more depth later, but understanding the foundations of our nature, temptation, and the perversion of that nature is important for us to understand redemption and the process of restoration. When we are fully restored, the relationship between men and God, men and women, and men and women with the creation, will all be part of a glorious paradise again.

DAY 24

Leaving and Cleaving

For this cause a man shall leave his father and his mother, and shall cleave to his wife; and they shall become one flesh (Genesis 1:24).

The relationship of fathers and mothers to their children is unique and special. For this reason the only commandment that had a promise attached to it was, **"Honor your father and your mother, that your days may be prolonged in the land which the LORD your God gives you" (Exodus 20:12).** Our longevity is dependent upon our honoring our fathers and mothers. Even so, when we marry, we must leave our fathers and mothers and cleave to our mates.

To **"leave"** our fathers and mothers does not mean we must cut off all relationship to them. We should relate to them, and honor them all the days of our lives. However, when we marry, our relationship to them must change. From that point, the primary communion of hearts that is designed to alleviate the loneliness must come from our mates, not our parents. Anything else will be a perversion of both relationships.

It is not natural for a man or woman to continue cleaving to their parents after they are married. If they do this, destruction of both relationships is possible, as well as the wounding of their own souls. There is a point in every man's life when he must become the man of his own home. There is a point in every woman's life when she must establish her own household. That point is marriage.

The authority of a father or mother over a son or daughter is cut at marriage. Fathers and mothers may always help their children with advice and wisdom when it is requested. However, after marriage, parental attempts to control will be destructive to the lives of their children. We were created to be free, and if we are mature enough to marry, we are mature enough to make the decisions and bear the responsibility of our choices. If we do not allow this basic responsibility to develop, it will make the ultimate accomplishment of our created purposes much more difficult.

In this scripture, we also see when the man and woman leave their father and mother to cleave to each other, they become one flesh. Sex before the commitment of marriage debases the wonderful purpose of sex, and will make the higher levels of union between the two much more difficult. Therefore, one of the greatest gifts that newlyweds can give to each other is virginity. The exploration and development of a fulfilling sex life together is not only a wonderful experience, it bonds the two together, strengthening the marriage like few other things can. Sex is not the highest level of communion, but it is a wonderful gift from our Creator to aid our quest for the highest levels of communion.

As parents, we must understand that anything we do to interfere in the relationship of our children with their spouses may save them from some short term mistakes, but will usually be very detrimental to them in the long run. As parents, we often do have more wisdom gained from past experiences. Sometimes it is hard for us to let our children go and do things which we know are not the best for them. However, to not let them grow in their relationship to each other, by facing such choices together, and dealing with the consequences whether they are good or bad, will hurt them more. They must learn to "cleave" to each other, and sometimes their mistakes can help them more in the long run. When our children marry, our relationship to them must change. In-law stress is a major destructive force in marriage. One of the primary forces that keeps young couples from learning to cleave to one another is the interference of their parents. Parents, for the sake of your children, when they marry, let them go.

In marriage, it is often a serious trial to learn how to leave our fathers and mothers, if our parents do not understand this basic issue. However, it must be done and we must cleave to our spouse, and yet still honor our fathers and mothers. Few are able to navigate this difficult course without a few bruises. Even so, it is essential for a truly fulfilling marriage. For this reason, it is usually good to emphasize the word "leave" your father and mother. If necessary, move as far away from them as you can to prevent the wrong kind of interference. It may be painful for a while, but it can be much more painful later if not done. Every new couple needs to establish their own household, and their own identity as a family. This is another essential if we are to walk in the freedom that is required to be who we were created to be.

DAY 25

Openness

And the man and his wife were both naked and were not ashamed (Genesis 2:25).

God established the relationship between men and women in a way that would help to preserve and enhance their relationship to Him and each other. All relationships are built upon trust. Trust is the bridge over which meaningful interchange takes place. The stronger the bridge, the more weight that can be carried across this bridge. You can have love, and you can have forgiveness, but if you do not have trust, it will be a shallow relationship.

When the man and woman were naked, it is implied that it was more than being without clothes. They trusted each other enough to be open and transparent with each other. This is the way that we were created to be, completely free and open with others, with nothing being hidden. This is the goal of marriage—two people who are completely open and free with each other.

That the man and woman were naked and "not ashamed," explains why they were able to be transparent and trusting with each other. Shame is one of the most destructive forces in a relationship because it causes us to begin hiding things from each other. Relationships that are begun and kept from the things that cause shame will be the strongest and most fulfilling. Therefore, true love will always be devoted to purity first, not the immediate gratification.

Shame destroys relationships between us and God, ourselves, and others. Shame is the result of sin. It is caused by doing things that we know are wrong. When we willfully sin, it causes us to want to hide. Sin begins to kill the free expression of our hearts, which distorts our personalities, and our potential.

God created us to be social creatures, thus needing fellowship with Him and with each other. Shame causes hiding from one another, and also results in the first thing that God said was not good—loneliness. Sin is not worth the price.

Like the tragedy of Adam and Eve, most seem to have to experience the consequences of sin before they will believe it. However, if we will choose to do what is right, determining we will not do the things that will cause us to have to hide anything, we will begin to experience the greatest freedom that we can ever know. We will also begin to see an amazing change in our relationships. Shame should be a red warning light to us that what we are doing is wrong, as we read in I John 1:6-7:

If we say that we have fellowship with Him and yet walk in the darkness, we lie and do not practice the truth;
but if we walk in the light as He Himself is in the light, we have fellowship with one another, and the blood of Jesus His Son cleanses us from all sin.

As stated, the Greek word translated **"fellowship"** in this text is *koinonia*. This word implies far more than just a casual friendship. It is a deep union. The word **"cleanses"** indicates more than just a removal of the consequences of our sin, but also the removal of shame. The restored fellowship we are supposed to have in Christ, is intended to remove the shame that entered with the fall. This will allow us to be sincere and candid with one another. If we are walking in the light as the Lord is in the light, we will have a fellowship that is so deep and real with Him and His people, that there will be nothing we have to hide from each other. If we say that we have this fellowship, but have things that we cannot bring into the light, we are lying (see I John 1:6).

If we have something in our lives that we are afraid will be uncovered, then we should get rid of it. Anything that we are afraid to have brought to the light is evil because it can only survive in darkness. We should also refrain from any kind of secret relationships, secret clubs, or organizations that are secretive. Such will not be light, but obviously contain darkness or they would not have to be kept secret. Of course, persecution may call for an exception to this, as there are places where Christians must meet together in secret for their safety. However, there is a great difference in organizations that are secretive, and those that are forced to be secret because of persecution.

We should also seek to be such trustworthy people that others feel free to share openly with us. Sometimes love requires discretion, and this **"love covers a multitude of sins" (I Peter 4:8)**. Above all, as we read in I John 2:28, **"And now, little children, abide in Him, so that when He appears, we may have confidence and not shrink away from Him in shame at His coming."** Such a hope will keep us pure.

DAY 26

The Question

Now the serpent was more crafty than any beast of the field which the LORD God had made. And he said to the woman, "Indeed, has God said, 'You shall not eat from any tree of the garden'?"

And the woman said to the serpent, "From the fruit of the trees of the garden we may eat;

but from the fruit of the tree which is in the middle of the garden, God has said, 'You shall not eat from it or touch it, lest you die'" (Genesis 3:1-3).

The first thing said about the serpent was that he was **"crafty."** Being crafty is different from being wise. Craftiness is usually devoted to finding brilliant ways to bend the rules. Contrary to this, Jesus came to fulfill the law. One of the fundamental ways we can distinguish those who are sent by God from those who are sent by the devil are: one is seeking ways to obey, and the other is seeking ways to avoid obedience and get away with it.

In his craftiness, the serpent did not boldly contradict the Lord's command at first, but just encouraged Eve to question it. There are good questions and there are bad ones. The good ones are motivated by faith, seeking to know the Lord's ways so that we can please Him. The bad ones are usually motivated by fear, or the desire to bend the rules. The serpent was trying to get the woman to question God in the wrong way, which is usually the first step into his deadly trap.

The woman's response to the serpent's question reveals the doorway to the disobedience the devil was seeking. She responded that the Lord commanded that they should not eat from the forbidden tree **"or touch it."** The Lord did not say anything about not touching it. Adding to the Word of God is just as wrong as taking away from it. This reveals that we esteem our own opinions as much as we do His Word. This was the sin of the Pharisees that led to holding their own traditions even above the Word of God.

As stated, there are good and bad questions, which can actually be the same question. Whether they are good or bad is determined by our motives. There was nothing wrong with Eve wanting to understand the Tree of Knowledge of Good and Evil. It was only wrong for her to eat from it. God created us with curiosity, which is the foundation of a seeking heart. However, we must always guard ourselves against the trap that Eve fell into, which is doubting God. He is true, just, and always has our best interests in mind. Anything that causes us to doubt Him will lead to evil. This often begins with a simple tendency to just want to bend the rules.

It is the Lord's delight to turn our weaknesses into strengths. It is the devil's delight to turn our strengths into weaknesses, or opportunities to cause us to fall. He will try to take a seeking heart and turn it into a cynical heart. A cynical heart questions everything from the perspective of doubt, rather than faith. This has caused the tragic fall of journalism in our own times, taking those who begin with a desire for truth and understanding, and sowing such a cynical attitude in them that they often become strongholds for the accuser of the brethren.

Watch out for "craftiness." Watch out for those who propose anything that conflicts with the clear Word of God. If we allow ourselves to be deceived by such reasoning, it will lead to a fall. As we are told in I Corinthians 15:33, **Do not be deceived: "Bad company corrupts good morals."** The church is called to be the highest form of fellowship on earth. The devil also knows very well that spiritual authority is multiplied with unity, and if even two people come into agreement, God will answer their prayers (see Matthew 18:19). The devil is, therefore, continually seeking to bring discord to fellowship. We must guard our fellowship against the inclusion of those who are constantly causing divisions, or causing God's little ones to stumble, as we are told in Romans 16:17-18:

> **Now I urge you, brethren, keep your eye on those who cause dissensions and hindrances contrary to the teaching which you learned, and turn away from them.**
> **For such men are slaves, not of our Lord Christ but of their own appetites; and by their smooth and flattering speech they deceive the hearts of the unsuspecting.**

Jude referred to these stumbling blocks as **"faultfinders"** (verse 16). We have a responsibility to protect the Lord's people from these.

At the same time, we must guard our own hearts against becoming cynical or closed to those the Lord may be seeking to join to us. The faultfinders and the stumbling blocks that the enemy sends to cause divisions will show their true natures quickly. We must remove them, and turn away from them, or they will do great damage to the fellowship of the saints. We must also do this in a way that does not close our hearts to legitimate correction from the authority that the Lord has established in His church.

DAY 27

The Trap

And the serpent said to the woman, "You surely shall not die!

"For God knows that in the day you eat from it your eyes will be opened, and you will be like God, knowing good and evil" (Genesis 3:4-5).

When the devil saw that the woman had already shown a subtle disrespect for God's command by adding to it, he then pushed her all of the way into the trap by boldly contradicting God. When Eve did not recoil at this, her fate was sealed. If we are prone to either add to or take away from the Word of God, we will be prime candidates for deception. If we do not take a stand against the blatant contradictions to God's Word, we will likewise be easy prey for the crafty.

In contrast to Eve, when Jesus was tempted by the devil, He took His stand on God's Word. The foundation of obedience is having it settled in our heart that God's Word is true. Whenever we are being tempted, we should flee to the Word of God and search for what the Bible says on the issue. It is very unlikely that Eve would have eaten the forbidden fruit if she had waited to ask God about the serpent's assertions. The Lord promises us that if we seek, we will find (see Matthew 7:7). He will teach us His ways if we seek Him. It is not wrong to take our questions to the Lord.

We should also note that the very first recorded lie of Satan was **"You surely shall not die."** This is still his basic lie, and the great deception that is the root of most false religions and beliefs. Yet, the Word of God is clear, **"For the wages of sin is death" (Romans 6:23).** Sin leads to death. It does not matter how crafty the philosophies or religions sound, if we believe anything other than God's Word, it will be our doom.

What is sin? It is disobeying God. He made us, and He knows what is best for us. He only established one rule for the first man and woman, and it was to protect them. He did not say to them that the day they ate from the fruit of the tree that He was going to kill them. He said that the day they ate from it, they would die. He knew that the fruit was poison. It was the fruit that would kill them, and it did. The Lord always has our best interests in mind. He has only designated those things as sin that will hurt us and His creation.

God has established guidelines for our lives. If we insist on bending the rules, it will result in our own destruction. These rules were not made just to frustrate us, but rather to keep us safe. Sin kills. Disobedience is sin, and it will always result in tragedy. Let us establish in our hearts that God is good, His ways are all righteous and true, and it is for our good that He has established the guidelines by which we should live. If we desire understanding, let us ask for the sake of becoming more perfect in our obedience.

We should also note that the Tree of Knowledge is in the middle of the Garden. This is also indicative of the primary result of eating its fruit—self-centeredness. When Adam and Eve ate from it, the first thing that they did was look at themselves. God-centeredness leads to life, while self-centeredness leads to death. The final push of the serpent to get the woman to eat the forbidden fruit was to get her to think that God was withholding something that she needed to feel complete. If the enemy can get us to focus on ourselves, especially on real or perceived personal inadequacies, we will then be easy prey for deception.

The enemy's strategy is to get us to look at ourselves, either the good or the bad, instead of looking to the adequacy of the Lord. By this we can usually recognize what the devil is planting in our hearts to lead us astray. Again, the fruit of the Tree of Knowledge kills by getting us to look at ourselves. In contrast to this, eating from The Tree of Life will result in our being Christ-centered. It is not who we are in Him, but who He is in us that leads to life and power.

We must know what sin is and be able to recognize it, but keeping our attention focused on the sin is not the path to a sin-free life. We do need to understand the schemes of the devil, but we must not keep our attention on him, or concern ourselves with knowing his ways too deeply. We are told in I Corinthians 11:31, **"But if we judged ourselves rightly, we should not be judged."** It is therefore right that we examine ourselves, but if we focus on self, we will fall.

We must focus our attention on the Lord and behold His glory, if we are going to be changed into His image. We must guard against any doctrine, or person, which tries to make us focus our attention on ourselves, the devil, or sin. The key word here is "focus." Follow those who are following Christ, growing in the knowledge of who He is, and getting ever closer to Him.

DAY 28

The Deception

When the woman saw that the tree was good for food, and that it was a delight to the eyes, and that the tree was desirable to make one wise (Genesis 3:6).

The deadly tree is called the Tree of the Knowledge of Good and Evil for a reason. The "good" side of the Tree of Knowledge is just as deadly as the "evil" side. When we seek to stand on "goodness" in place of the cross of Jesus Christ, it is an affront to the cross, an affront to God, and is just as much a root of the rebellion of mankind as the evil. The good side of this tree is probably responsible for as much death as the evil side. The good side is more deceptive, which is why it appeared that it was the good side of the fruit that appealed to Eve.

The fruit looked like it was good to eat. This puts another subtle question in Eve's mind. Why would God withhold something good from her? Many young people fall into this same trap with sex. They think if it feels good, and does not hurt anyone, what's wrong with it? It does hurt someone...you! It will hurt your relationship to your spouse by placing a tragic weakness in the very foundation of your marriage. It will hurt many throughout their lives with the burden of lust, rather than the freedom to love. The very day you eat from that tree, death will start to work in your life. It looks good, but its fruit is poison.

Then it says that the fruit was a **"delight to the eyes**." Isn't it strange how it went from looking good to being "delightful?" The more we look at sin, the more it will appeal to us. Jesus said in Matthew 6:22-23:

"The lamp of the body is the eye; if therefore your eye is clear, your whole body will be full of light.
"But if your eye is bad, your whole body will be full of darkness. If therefore the light that is in you is darkness, how great is the darkness!

Sin almost always begins with looking. Then if we look long enough it will be turned into lust. **"Then when lust has conceived, it gives birth to sin; and when sin is accomplished, it brings forth**

death" (James 1:15). It is much easier to keep the devil out of the house than it is to get him out once he is in. Resisting sin begins with controlling our eyes.

Job said, **"I have made a covenant with my eyes; How then could I gaze at a virgin?" (Job 31:1)** Job made a covenant with his eyes not to look upon that which might cause him to lust. We must do the same. The eye is the lamp of the body. If we are constantly looking at things that we should not, we will constantly be filled with lust. If we determine to only look upon that which is good and upright, our hearts will be filled with that which is good and upright.

Eve listened to the devil, then looked at the sin until it became "delightful." Then came the clincher, it was **"desirable to make one wise."** There is good wisdom and bad wisdom. There is good, bad, and deadly knowledge. The Lord commended those in the church of Thyatira who had not known the **"deep things of Satan" (Revelation 2:24).** We must understand the schemes of the devil, but we must resist the temptation to understand the depths of evil.

We read in Philippians 4:8: **"Finally, brethren, whatever is true, whatever is honorable, whatever is right, whatever is pure, whatever is lovely, whatever is of good repute, if there is any excellence and if anything worthy of praise, let your mind dwell on these things."** In II Corinthians 10:5 it says, **"We are destroying speculations and every lofty thing raised up against the knowledge of God, and we are taking every thought captive to the obedience of Christ."**

The mind is wonderful, but we must learn to discipline ourselves and our thoughts. There is a saying that "we are what we eat." There is truth to this statement, just as Adam and Eve found out in the Garden. They took on the nature of the tree from which they ate. We, too, will tend to take on the nature of what we allow into our minds. We must choose what we are going to eat, and what we are going to allow into our minds and hearts. We must discern the books, television, music, and anything else that we are partaking of. Are they feeding the lusts of the flesh, or Christlikeness?

Remember that the choice is ours. Choose wisely. Choose life by choosing to continually partake of words that lead to life. Let us also choose life by always speaking words that give life. We read before from Ephesians 4:29: **"Let no unwholesome word proceed from your mouth, but only such a word as is good for edification according to the need of the moment, that it may give grace to those who hear."**

DAY 29

The Fall

She took from its fruit and ate; and she gave also to her husband with her, and he ate (Genesis 3:6).

If we listen to the devil, and give serious consideration to what he says, we will almost surely fall into his trap and sin. Those who fall into sin almost never do so because of a single, instantaneous temptation. It is usually a subtle, slow process of looking at something, dwelling on it, rationalizing it, and then when our defenses have been stripped away, the trap is sprung.

After the sin, the consequences began to immediately show in Adam and Eve's relationship to each other. Even though they had sinned together, there was an immediate barrier between them that had not been there before. Shame entered their relationship, and shame always brings division. The freedom and openness that they had known with each other were gone forever. Sin destroys relationships and turns life into death. It will almost always be appealing to our senses, and maybe even our intellect, but its fruit will always be bitter.

The Scriptures are very clear about sin. Murder, adultery, and stealing are some of the obvious ones. We are also told in the New Testament that even to be angry with a brother is sin (Matthew 5:22). We are also told in James 4:17, **"Therefore, to one who knows the right thing to do, and does not do it, to him it is sin."** There are sins of commission, which are evil things we do, and sins of omission, which is not doing good when it is in our power to do it.

Basically, sin is disobedience to God. Sin is always the result of selfishness in some form, and it will always result in further self-centeredness that separates us from God and one another. Regardless of how appealing it looks, sin destroys.

Even so consider yourselves to be dead to sin, but alive to God in Christ Jesus.
Therefore do not let sin reign in your mortal body that you should obey its lusts,

> **and do not go on presenting the members of your body to sin as instruments of unrighteousness; but present yourselves to God as those alive from the dead, and your members as instruments of righteousness to God (Romans 6:11-13).**

We flee from sin by pursuing righteousness. We flee from hatred by pursuing love. We flee from fears by pursuing faith. We flee from impatience by seeking to be more patient. As Romans 12:21 states, **"Do not be overcome by evil, but overcome evil with good."** We must always seek to displace the evil in our hearts with good.

Righteousness is a gift and a treasure. True righteousness is never "self-righteousness" because true righteousness is not in us, but in Christ. We are only righteous to the degree that we abide in Him. Our pursuit must be to abide in Him in all things. God is love, so if we abide in Him, we will love. He does not fear anything, so if we abide in Him, we will be free from fear, etc. Our goal is not to just grow in love, but walk in more of God's love. We do not want to have less fear, but rather have the faith that comes from seeing from the Lord's perspective, which is at the right hand of the Father. When we see who Jesus is, and where He sits, we will have faith.

We should replace the negative things in our lives with the positive aspects of Christ. If television is a problem for us, rather than just determining not to watch television, we should pursue something positive with our time to replace watching television. We might start with a 30-day television fast, but have something positive to do during the time that we normally watch television, such as attending a Bible study, ministering to others, reading, etc. If we just do away with the sin, it leaves a hole that the enemy will easily return to if the void is not filled. We must overcome sin by replacing it with the Lord's will.

If we will actively pursue the Lord, we will be far less likely to fall into the traps that the enemy has set to cause us to stumble. We must have a vision of growing in the grace, fruit, and power of the Spirit. I Corinthians 14:1 exhorts us to, **"Pursue love, yet desire earnestly spiritual gifts, but especially that you may prophesy."** Love must be pursued. Those who just desire spiritual gifts seldom receive them, but those who "earnestly desire" them will. We must desire the things of God enough to seek them earnestly. The Lord promised in Jeremiah 29:13: **"And you will seek Me and find Me, when you search for Me with all your heart."**

DAY 30

The Cover Up

Then the eyes of both of them were opened, and they knew that they were naked; and they sewed fig leaves together and made themselves loin coverings (Genesis 3:7).

Here the sin goes a little deeper. As we have studied, Adam and Eve's first response to sin was for them to look at themselves. Self-centeredness is the poison from the Tree of Knowledge that kills. We were created to be God-centered. The restoration process through which our minds are renewed and we are delivered from our sin nature, comes from seeing the glory of God, as we read in II Corinthians 3:18:

But we all, with unveiled face beholding as in a mirror, the glory of the Lord, are being transformed into the same image from glory to glory, just as from the Lord, the Spirit.

Deliverance from sin comes from turning away from sin and self-centeredness to become God-centered again. It is not our goal to just find out who we are in Christ, but rather who He is in us. The former can still be self-centeredness, even though it can be mixed with many good motives.

If we are going to be changed into His image, we must behold His glory with an **"unveiled face."** Veils are the defense mechanisms that the sin nature compels us to wear to protect ourselves. They are an extension of the coverings that Adam and Eve made after their sin. Sin causes us to be self-aware and self-protective to the point where we are afraid for anyone to see us as we are. These veils must be stripped away so that we can see the Lord as He is, and so that we can be real with one another.

To be real is to walk in truth, and to relate to others without pretension. By repenting of sin, the process is begun, which goes from **"glory to glory."** The more we allow the veils, the defense mechanisms, to be stripped away, the more of His glory we will see, and the more we will become like Him.

When we sin, the first tendency we have is to cover, hide, or rationalize the sin. When this occurs, death is released against us, and it will begin to drain life from us. Repentance begins with acknowledging the sin, calling it what it is, and taking responsibility for it.

If we say that we have fellowship with Him and yet walk in the darkness, we lie and do not practice the truth;

but if we walk in the light as He Himself is in the light, we have fellowship with one another, and the blood of Jesus His Son cleanses us from all sin.

If we say that we have no sin, we are deceiving ourselves, and the truth is not in us.

If we confess our sins, He is faithful and righteous to forgive us our sins and to cleanse us from all unrighteousness.

If we say that we have not sinned, we make Him a liar, and His word is not in us (I John 1:6-10).

As stated, the natural response to sin is to hide it, pretend there was no sin, or rationalize the sin. All of these responses only deepen sin's grip on us, and open us to further deception. The answer is not to cover the sin, but rather acknowledge it, fleeing to the cross for forgiveness and healing from the wound the sin has caused. As the scripture above states, we must confess our sins in order to be forgiven, and then He can cleanse us.

Judas was called "incorrigible," or beyond help. What made him incorrigible was not that He betrayed the Lord, but that he hung himself. We have probably all betrayed the Lord because He said that as we have done it to the least of His people, we have done it to Him. (see Matthew 25:40). Judas could have been forgiven, but instead of fleeing to the Lord for forgiveness, he tried to pay the price for his own sin. By doing that, he was beyond the Lord's help. We, too, are beyond His help when we either cover our sin and pretend it does not exist, or insist on paying the price for it ourselves. These are an affront to the cross of Jesus, which alone can pay for our sins. James 3:2 says, **"For we all stumble in many ways."**

Let us not respond to sin by trying to cover it, or "hanging ourselves," but rather flee to the grace of God at the cross. Jesus died to pay for that sin. To not allow Him to pay the price for our sin is to reject His great grace. If we are going to be free, and grow in the trust that all relationships are based on, we must trust the cross.

DAY 31

The Delusion

And they heard the sound of the LORD God walking in the garden in the cool of the day, and the man and his wife hid themselves from the presence of the LORD God among the trees of the garden.

Then the LORD God called to the man, and said to him, "Where are you?" (Genesis 3:8-9).

It is interesting that when the man and woman's "eyes were opened" they became foolish. No one can hide from God, though it is probable that all men have tried to from time to time. He is the All-Seeing-One, and the All-Knowing-One. He knows the number of hairs on our head (see Matthew 10:30). One thing that we can be sure of—when the Omniscient God asks a question, it is not because He is seeking information! When He asked Adam where He was, it was for Adam's sake. This is a question that echoes throughout the ages, calling man to understand how foolish it is to hide from Him.

Even so, every human being will spend his life trying to hide from God if the cross is not embraced. Even religious pursuits can be an attempt to hide who we really are from God. We can even use the seeming pursuit of God to assuage our own consciences so that we feel better, even though we are only increasing our deception. Such religious pursuits are always the attempts of man to try to meet with God on man's own terms. It is just another form of trying to hide from Him, and He is never fooled by them.

In such cases, we will only accept Him in the way we can understand Him. What we cannot understand, we reject. However, He is far too big for us to understand. It is the ultimate human arrogance for us to think that we can understand God, though it is the most righteous quest of all to seek to know Him. We must seek to know Him with the understanding that He will always be greater than our natural minds can comprehend. We will always see in part and know in part. Even so, to learn anything about His ways is more valuable than all of the treasures on earth.

77

James 4:6 states, **Therefore it says, "God is opposed to the proud, but gives grace to the humble."** It is pride to think that we can cover ourselves, hide from God, and understand Him on our own. Such prideful human searching for the divine, is one of the greatest delusions of all. The only way that we can understand Him is for Him to reveal Himself. If we really want to see Him as He is, we must humble ourselves and beg for His mercy.

The beginning of humility is to stop trying to cover ourselves and hide. Sin has caused us to turn away from Him. True repentance is more than just turning away from sin—it is turning to God.

Profound pride causes us to think that we can fix ourselves. Humility leads to His grace when we simply turn to Him, coming to Him just as we are, and asking Him to fix us. The humility that releases His grace is the acknowledgment that we need Him. Those who do this are never turned away.

The antidote for our tendency to hide is not just seeking to expose ourselves, but rather simply seeking God. When we sin, we must not run from Him, but rather to Him. He already knows what we have done, and He knows where we are hiding. As a father, my respect and appreciation for my children grows when they come to me with a confession of a transgression, rather than me finding out about it. I may still have to discipline them if they come to me with a confession, but my trust in them is increased even though they have made a mistake.

One of the greatest liberations we can ever experience is to know that everything is in the light. We will sleep more peacefully when we are not worried about someone finding out something about us that is hidden. Whenever we are tempted to hide, let us resolve to seek the Lord with even more diligence, always remembering the great promise of Hebrews 4:15-16:

> **And there is no creature hidden from His sight, but all things are open and laid bare to the eyes of Him with whom we have to do.**
> **For we do not have a high priest who cannot sympathize with our weaknesses, but one who has been tempted in all things as we are, yet without sin.**
> **Let us therefore draw near with confidence to the throne of grace, that we may receive mercy and may find grace to help in time of need.**

DAY 32

Fear

And he (Adam) said, "I heard the sound of Thee in the garden, and I was afraid because I was naked; so I hid myself" (Genesis 3:10).

The first mention of fear in the Bible is in the above verse. There is a pure and holy fear of God, and there is an unholy fear. This is the unholy fear of God that leads to further corruption of the soul, and causes us to run from Him instead of to Him.

The holy fear of God would never cause us to attempt to hide from Him. The holy fear of God is rooted in the knowledge that He is God and no one can hide from Him. It acknowledges that He is all-knowing, and we at best know very little. The holy fear of God is the **"beginning of wisdom" (Proverbs 9:10)** because it acknowledges that we need help from Him to know anything accurately.

The unholy fear of God is rooted in the poisonous fruit of the Tree of Knowledge of Good and Evil. This fear is not rooted so much in who God is, but in our own self-centeredness. This is the fear that causes us to try to hide from God and one another. This causes the facades and pretensions that so dominate the relationships of fallen men.

Unholy fear is rooted especially in the fear of rejection. Because man was created to have fellowship with God and one another, rejection is one of the most painful human experiences, and one of the most crippling fears that dominates the human race. Rejection will either cause one to cower in hiding, or try to dominate others so you will always be the first to do the rejecting. Therefore, it takes great faith in God to come out of hiding in spite of our own nakedness. It takes great faith to be vulnerable, but this is the first step toward redemption and restoration.

Jesus was the Lord of Glory and yet He emptied Himself to become a frail human child. He made Himself utterly vulnerable, even allowing corrupt, fallen men to beat and humiliate Him before submitting to the ultimate humiliation of the cross. He became vulnerable to us so we would forever understand how much He loves us. When we begin to truly behold the cross, we will begin to come out of hiding. The cross alone will free us from our deepest fears and allow us to start being real again.

Fear was introduced to man when he ate the forbidden fruit. Generally, fear is one of the biggest open doors through which the evil one enters into the lives of people. The devil controls men with fear; but the Lord leads men with faith. This battle for the heart of man is basically the determination of whether fear or faith will rule.

Faith begins by knowing God's acceptance of us through the cross. This acceptance has nothing to do with what we have done or have not done, but on what Jesus did for us. One of the great testimonies of God's grace is the way it has been extended to even the most grotesque murderers and transgressors. It is understandable that men would be skeptical of the notable death row conversions, but the grace we can find at the cross is enough to cover any who seek refuge in Him. In fact, the Lord Himself said that those who are forgiven much will love Him much. Therefore, as we read in Romans 5:19-21:

> **For as through the one man's disobedience the many were made sinners, even so through the obedience of the One the many will be made righteous.**
> **And the Law came in that the transgression might increase; but where sin increased, grace abounded all the more,**
> **that, as sin reigned in death, even so grace might reign through righteousness to eternal life through Jesus Christ our Lord.**

Where sin abounds, grace abounds even more. Does this mean we should sin so that His grace will abound and we will love Him more? This is an ultimate deception—just as Paul addressed this question in the verses that followed, Romans 6:1-4:

> **What shall we say then? Are we to continue in sin that grace might increase?**
> **May it never be! How shall we who died to sin still live in it?**
> **Or do you not know that all of us who have been baptized into Christ Jesus have been baptized into His death?**
> **Therefore we have been buried with Him through baptism into death, in order that as Christ was raised from**

the dead through the glory of the Father, so we too might walk in newness of life.

If we have light in us, we will walk in the light, not in darkness. However, when we do make a mistake, let us flee to His grace and love, which is more abundant than we could ever exhaust.

Day 33

The Voices

And He said, "Who told you that you were naked? Have you eaten from the tree of which I commanded you not to eat?" (Genesis 3:11)

It is interesting to note that Adam and Eve did not think it was strange that a serpent spoke to them. From this we can deduct that before the fall, man could communicate freely with the creatures, and they with him. The fall caused the corruption of one of man's greatest gifts—the gift of communication.

It is now estimated that even the greatest human genius only uses about 10 percent of his brain. Why has the other 90 percent become dormant? What was it used for in the beginning? It is also interesting that man now lives an average of less than 10 percent as long as the first men. As the process of the fall proceeded and deepened, man's life-span shrank proportionately, and so did his mental capacity.

Likewise, Adam and Eve fell to sin and death because they listened to the wrong voice, the voice of the serpent. The devil does still speak to us, and tries to deceive us so that we will give ourselves to sin and rebellion. We must challenge every voice that seeks to lead us into beliefs or actions that are in contradiction to God's Word. To counter this, we must develop our own ability to hear the Lord, to understand what He is saying, and to obey His voice.

Those who do not know God believe that it is a form of insanity to think that you have heard the voice of God. However, the Scriptures testify that we are not truly the Lord's sheep unless we know His voice, as we read in John 10:4-5 where the Lord refers to Himself as the good Shepherd:

"When he puts forth all his own, he goes before them, and the sheep follow him because they know his voice.
"And a stranger they simply will not follow, but will flee from him, because they do not know the voice of strangers."

The Lord did not say that the lambs knew His voice, but rather the sheep. Sheep will follow their shepherd while the lambs will follow the sheep. Likewise, the spiritually young usually do need to follow more mature believers until they have grown to know the Lord's voice for themselves. However, it should be the goal of every believer to know the Lord's voice, and be able to quickly and easily distinguish His voice from all of the other voices in the world.

Many who claim to be believers assert that the Lord no longer speaks because He has given us the Bible, but the Bible itself refutes this false doctrine. We are told that the Lord never changes, and that He **"is the same yesterday and today, yes and forever" (Hebrews 13:8).** He is not an author who just wrote one book and then retired! He is alive and still relates to His people personally the same ways that He always has.

The Bible is a wonderful gift, and should always be the basis of all doctrine and teaching. However, the Lord does not just relate to His people as the Teacher. He is also our Shepherd, and the sheep follow Him **"because they *know* His voice" (John 10:4).** He is also the Prophet, and He still speaks through His people.

He is also the Bridegroom. The quality of any relationship can be measured by the quality of its communication. What bride would like to hear from her bridegroom that he has written a book for her, and the only way he is going to communicate with her again, is for her to read the book and learn all that he expects from her? It would be a dead relationship. The doctrine that the Lord only speaks through the Bible to His people today, has likewise, brought forth many churches that are dead because they are, as we read in II Timothy 3:5, **"holding to a form of godliness, although they have denied its power...,"** and as the verse continues, we should **"avoid such men as these."**

DAY 34

The Fall Deepens

And the man said, "The woman whom Thou gavest to be with me, she gave me from the tree, and I ate."

Then the LORD God said to the woman, "What is this you have done?" And the woman said, "The serpent deceived me, and I ate" (Genesis 3:12-13).

The man said that it was the woman's fault. The woman said that it was the serpent's fault. Since God put the serpent in the garden, she was in fact implying that the whole thing was God's fault. Man has been trying to blame God for his problems ever since. This only leads to a deeper human depravity.

The three major perversions caused by the fall were: 1) self-centeredness, 2) hiding, and 3) blame-shifting. If man had stopped at any of these points and begun turning back to God, the fall would not likely have led to the depth of corruption to the human race that it did. If we will stop before this progression has fully developed, and turn to God, it will prevent us from likewise falling into a deeper problem.

When anyone sins, they will usually follow these same steps. First, they become self-centered, which causes them to try to hide, and start blame-shifting. The deeper the corruption, the more difficult it is to be helped out of our problems. The usual procedure for dealing with sin was dramatically demonstrated by President Clinton's response to the exposure of his affair. First he tried to hide it. Then, in a most interesting television address to the nation about the issue, he tried to actually pin some of the blame on the harassment of the special council. The whole nation seemed to recognize this fallacy with our President, but how often do we recognize it in ourselves?

The Lord does not forgive excuses; He forgives sin. He is always ready to forgive us if we repent. To repent is to acknowledge that it is our fault, and we made a mistake. Blame-shifting instead of repentance is to further build the barriers between ourselves and God, and ourselves and others. It takes humility to admit that we were wrong, but God gives His grace to the humble. Genuine humility is genuine repentance.

We can blame our mistakes on other people, or on our environment, but it will never deliver us from the consequences of those mistakes. There is no genuine repentance until we accept the responsibility for our actions. Only genuine repentance results in forgiveness and reconciliation, with God and men.

In recent history, fallen men have released a seemingly continuous stream of philosophies and psychologies that try to shift the blame for the depravities of man to things such as environment, how we were raised, etc. It is true that these things do have an influence on us, and can have a significant impact on the makeup of our character, but the way out of this maze is not to blame someone else, but to start taking personal responsibility for our problems and failures.

The environment is not the problem. The Lord put man in a perfect environment and he still sinned. If the environment was the problem, then the Lord would have needed to just redeem the environment and not man. The Lord gave authority over the environment to man. When man is redeemed, man will then be able to properly relate to, and change his environment. This is simply a matter of putting the proverbial horse in front of the cart where it belongs.

Practically speaking, we should always view problems with our situation, or environment, and highlight the things that are wrong with us that needs to be changed. Because God's purpose is to fully redeem and restore us from the consequences of the fall, we should always first look for the answer to our problems as a needed change in us. In almost every case the answer can be summed up in one word, "love." As we are told in I Corinthians 13:8, **"Love never fails."** Love will always be found at the root of every solution. If we would love more, it would change most of the situations that we view as our problems.

The Lord began changing the world by loving it enough to die for it. We can also begin changing our world when we begin loving those around us enough to lay down our lives, and our self-interests for their sakes. Instead of blame-shifting, let us acknowledge our own sin, taking responsibility for it, and seek the grace of God to love those around us, instead of blaming them for our problems. When we begin to truly love in this way, paradise will begin to return.

Day 35

The Curse on the Serpent

And the LORD God said to the serpent, "Because you have done this, cursed are you more than all cattle, And more than every beast of the field; On your belly shall you go, And dust shall you eat All the days of your life;

And I will put enmity Between you and the woman, And between your seed and her seed; He shall bruise you on the head, And you shall bruise him on the heel" (Genesis 3:14-15).

The first curse came upon the serpent. We know the serpent was the devil (see Revelation 12:9). That he was cursed to travel on his belly on the earth, seems to also be a metaphor of how he was cast out of heaven down to the earth. Of all the regions of the universe, the devil has been restricted to the earth.

Compared to the rest of creation, the earth is like a grain of sand to the oceans of the sea. We are but a speck of dust to the rest of creation. All the evil in the universe is imprisoned on this little planet, while God's righteousness prevails over the billions of galaxies and the heavenly realm that is even more expansive. The devil and all of his evil followers may prevail here for a time, but compared to eternity, it is like a brief moment. The domain of God is of unfathomable greatness and expanse. As C.S. Lewis once wrote, "the Lord's domain is so great that if all of the evil deeds and thoughts on earth and in hell were combined and hurled into heaven, they probably would not even have the weight to register as a single thought on the least of the creatures there."

To those of us who live here where the devil and his hosts have been cast, it seems that evil prevails over all. Therefore, we must keep things in perspective. He is certainly crawling on his belly, lower than all of the other creatures.

The serpent was also told that he would eat dust. Because man was created from the dust, in Scripture this often represents the flesh of man, or his carnal nature. From that time, the devil has fed off the carnal nature of man. Every time we give in to following the flesh instead of the spirit, we are feeding the evil one. Paul wrote in Romans 8:5-11:

> **For those who are according to the flesh set their minds on the things of the flesh, but those who are according to the Spirit, the things of the Spirit.**
>
> **For the mind set on the flesh is death, but the mind set on the Spirit is life and peace,**
>
> **because the mind set on the flesh is hostile toward God; for it does not subject itself to the law of God, for it is not even able to do so;**
>
> **and those who are in the flesh cannot please God.**
>
> **However, you are not in the flesh but in the Spirit, if indeed the Spirit of God dwells in you. But if anyone does not have the Spirit of Christ, he does not belong to Him.**
>
> **And if Christ is in you, though the body is dead because of sin, yet the spirit is alive because of righteousness.**
>
> **But if the Spirit of Him who raised Jesus from the dead dwells in you, He who raised Christ Jesus from the dead will also give life to your mortal bodies through His Spirit who indwells you.**

Because the devil feeds on the carnal nature of man, when we fall into carnality we are feeding and strengthening his domain in our life. We must learn to feed our spirits, not our carnal nature. We feed our spirits by keeping what we read, watch, or even think about, pure. Our spirits will grow stronger by fellowship, sharing the gospel, and exercising the spiritual gifts that we have been given. We are told in I John 3:7-8,10-11:

> **Little children, let no one deceive you; the one who practices righteousness is righteous, just as He is righteous;**
>
> **the one who practices sin is of the devil; for the devil has sinned from the beginning. The Son of God appeared for this purpose, that He might destroy the works of the devil.**
>
> **By this the children of God and the children of the devil are obvious: anyone who does not practice righteousness is not of God, nor the one who does not love his brother.**

For this is the message which you have heard from the beginning, that we should love one another;

We cannot partake of Christ and go on living in the ways of the evil one. If we are Christ's, we will pursue righteousness by love. The whole law is fulfilled in the two great commandments, loving God and loving one another. If we pursue the course of love in all we do, we will grow in the nature of the Lord, because God is love.

DAY 36

The Curse on the Woman

To the woman He said, "I will greatly multiply Your pain in childbirth, In pain you shall bring forth children; Yet your desire shall be for your husband, And he shall rule over you" (Genesis 3:16).

The Lord created the man and woman to procreate, but childbirth was not intended to be painful. Because of the fall, pain was "greatly" multiplied, resulting from the disharmony that had entered the world through sin. Before sin, all creatures lived in harmony. There was cooperation between the creation on earth and their appointed rulers. Now there was conflict, which always leads to pain.

As a part of the curse, the man was appointed to rule over the woman. This is an increasingly unpopular truth, mostly because of the tragic oppression and abuse of authority by men over women. Even so, the Lord has a "woman's liberation movement" that will greatly transcend the one that the enemy has perpetrated to try to preempt and sidetrack it. The promulgation of true spiritual authority will be the liberation of everyone.

True spiritual authority does not bind and oppress, but it liberates. **"Where the Spirit of the Lord is, there is liberty" (II Corinthians 3:17).** True spiritual authority is a protective covering that brings freedom to those who are under it, to be what they were created to be. This authority is not for the purpose of subjugation, but rather to serve and free those who are under its covering. When true spiritual authority is restored to the church as it was originally intended, it will free both men and women to be all that God created them to be. Authority will be exercised in love, not anger, and those who are under truly loving authority will be the most free people on the earth.

It is apparent that the man did have a leadership role before the fall because the command to not eat from the Tree of Knowledge was given to the man. But there is a difference in "leading" and "ruling." Even though they were to rule over the creation, it seems that it was not originally intended for men to rule over other men or women.

Because of the fall, the harmony had been broken. Rulership had to be established to keep the creation from falling into complete chaos until there could be a restoration from the fall.

Rulership is now needed to keep order. Even so, true authority that is working for the redemption and restoration of man is love demonstrated. It is not domineering, though it may at times be decisive and steadfast. It is liberating when authority is exercised for the sake of those under it. This type of authority is rare, even in the church. Even so, we must pursue true authority until it is recovered. That is why we are told in Ephesians 5:22-28:

> **Wives, be subject to your own husbands, as to the Lord.**
>
> **For the husband is the head of the wife, as Christ also is the head of the church, He Himself being the Savior of the body.**
>
> **But as the church is subject to Christ, so also the wives ought to be to their husbands in everything.**
>
> **Husbands, love your wives, just as Christ also loved the church and gave Himself up for her;**
>
> **that He might sanctify her, having cleansed her by the washing of water with the word,**
>
> **that He might present to Himself the church in all her glory, having no spot or wrinkle or any such thing; but that she should be holy and blameless.**
>
> **So husbands ought also to love their own wives as their own bodies. He who loves his own wife loves himself.**

The marriage relationship was intended to be a reflection of the love and union between Christ and His church. Until the relationship between men and women have been restored to this, redemption will not be fully worked into our lives.

The woman was taken out of man's side because that was the place she was to have, beside him. They were created differently in many ways and to have different roles, but this did not make one more important than the other. Men were created to carry the burden of certain types of authority, while women have more authority than men in other areas. Even so, authority in the kingdom of God is for serving, not being served. Our goal must be to become the families that truly reflect the relationship between Christ and His church. Then men will look at Christian men and know that this was what they were created to be. Women will look at Christian women and know that this is what they were created to be. Through this, all will begin to perceive just what the Lord intended in His own relationship to the church.

DAY 37

The Curse on the Man

Then to Adam He said, "Because you have listened to the voice of your wife, and have eaten from the tree about which I commanded you, saying, 'You shall not eat from it'; Cursed is the ground because of you; In toil you shall eat of it all the days of your life.

"Both thorns and thistles it shall grow for you; and you shall eat the plants of the field;

By the sweat of your face you shall eat bread, till you return to the ground, because from it you were taken; for you are dust, and to dust you shall return" (Genesis 3:17-19).

Paul, the apostle, wrote in I Timothy 2:14: **"And it was not Adam who was deceived, but the woman being quite deceived, fell into transgression."** The woman was deceived, but Adam knew what he was doing when he chose to sin, which is far more sinister. History testifies that even if women may be more prone to being deceived than men, men may know that something is evil and still do it. The great evils that have been done in the world were almost all done by men. In general, men may have the discernment to know that something is wrong, but women have the heart to refuse to do wrong if they know it. The Lord so composed men and women that they need each other if they are to stay on the path of life.

We also see that the ground was cursed because of the man. He had been given authority to rule over the earth, so when he fell, all that was under his authority fell. Disharmony and death spread to all because of the man. Because of this, he could now only draw from the earth by **"toil."** Remember that man was created to labor, but there is a difference between labor and toil. Labor is work, but toil is work that can only be accomplished with great or painful effort. Now, the world that the man had been given to rule over would resist him in everything he tried to do. The harmony, the communication, the fellowship of man with the Creator, and man with the creation, was profoundly damaged by his sin.

In Acts 3:20-21, Peter made a remarkable statement about the return of the Lord: **"and that He may send Jesus, the Christ appointed for you, whom heaven must receive until the period of restoration of all things about which God spoke by the mouth of His holy prophets from ancient time."** Jesus is called "the last Adam" by Paul because He is going to restore all that was lost by the first Adam's fall. Through the redemption of the cross, and the resurrection life of Christ, harmony, communication, and fellowship between man and God, man and man, and man and the creation, will be restored. As the redemption and restoration of Christ begins to work in our lives, we should begin to experience all of these. When this harmony has been restored, even our labor will not meet continual resistance, but will be fulfilling, and much more fruitful.

After the fall, men quickly fell into deeper and deeper depravity. Authority was increasingly perverted and oppressive, and therefore, opposition from the creation increased. When we are redeemed and born again into Christ, the "last Adam," we must go through a process where our minds are renewed. As our minds are renewed, we are restored to the place of harmony with God and the creation. As we are renewed in rulership, or the exercise of authority, we will also be changed.

All relationships are built on trust. In our fallen nature, we exercise authority for our own selfish reasons. As we are changed, and begin to grow in the love of God, authority is exercised for the sake of others. As authority is exercised in love, the bridge of trust is built step by step. Because of trust, the resistance of those under the authority of man, which includes the whole earth, will begin to lessen. By this, even productivity and fruitfulness will increase. The curse of toil is removed, as we are restored to our original state.

Therefore, understanding authority is crucial to the process of restoration. Jesus is the One who is above all rule and authority and power. We only have true spiritual authority to the degree that we abide in Him. He used His authority to empty Himself, fully identifying with us by becoming one of us, and then laying down His life for our salvation. As we come to abide in Him, we will use the authority entrusted to us in the same way. We will use it to lay down our own interests to serve the interests of others. We will lower ourselves in order to lift others up. In everything we do, we will be looking for the redemptive purposes of God and the restoration of all that was lost through the fall.

Just the very word "authority" carries the negative odor of the wounds that have been the result of authoritarianism. There is a natural resistance to authority, and rebellion is in the heart of every fallen creature. However, this will not be overcome with authoritarianism, but with the true spiritual authority that is rooted and grounded in love. Love serves.

DAY 38

The Covering

Now the man called his wife's name Eve, because she was the mother of all the living.
And the LORD God made garments of skin for Adam and his wife, and clothed them (Genesis 3:20-21).

This is considered the first prophecy of the atonement sacrifice of Christ. Adam and Eve had tried to cover themselves, but it was not adequate. Then the Lord made a covering for them by shedding the blood of an innocent animal, prophesying of the atonement that Jesus would make by shedding His blood for our sins.

There is nothing we can do to cover our sins. Our good works will never balance the evil and make us acceptable to God, or cover the shame and wounding that sin does to our soul. Only the Lord can cover our sins. For us to even try to cover ourselves is an affront to the cross of Jesus, by which our redemption was purchased.

Just as Adam and Eve's first response to their sin was to look at themselves, feel naked, and then try to cover themselves and hide, we can still go through the same process even after we become Christians and have the knowledge of the cross. However, regardless of how we feel, we must run to God when we sin, not away from Him. The price that He paid is enough to cover even our worse sins. When we refuse to go to the cross, and try to carry the guilt ourselves, we are saying that the cross was not enough, and this sin is so great that we will have to pay the price ourselves. This is a tragic delusion, and a pride that is not only an insult to the cross of Jesus, but a fundamental departure from the faith that the cross is enough for our salvation. We are assured in I John 1:7-9:

but if we walk in the light as He Himself is in the light, we have fellowship with one another, and the blood of Jesus His Son cleanses us from all sin.
If we say that we have no sin, we are deceiving ourselves, and the truth is not in us.

If we confess our sins, He is faithful and righteous to forgive us our sins and to cleanse us from all unrighteousness.

These scriptures clearly state that His blood cleanses us from *all* sin and from *all* unrighteousness. For us to consider we must do penance for our sins is an affront to the cross of Jesus. It is a tragic deception to think that the cross is not enough, and that we can do something to add to the work of the cross to pay for our own sins. We can never cover ourselves, but we can always be assured that the covering He provided for our sins is enough. We read in Ephesians 1:7-8:

In Him we have redemption through His blood, the forgiveness of our trespasses, according to the riches of His grace, which He lavished upon us.

In Ephesians 2:13 we are told, **"But now in Christ Jesus you who formerly were far off have been brought near by the blood of Christ."** This states a basic purpose of the cross, which is more than reconciling us to God, but also bringing us back to Himself in the close, intimate relationship that He originally intended to have with men. He wants to bring us *near*. This is also stated in Hebrews 10:19-22:

Since therefore, brethren, we have confidence to enter the holy place by the blood of Jesus,
by a new and living way which He inaugurated for us through the veil, that is, His flesh,
and since we have a great priest over the house of God,
let us draw near with a sincere heart in full assurance of faith, having our hearts sprinkled clean from an evil conscience and our bodies washed with pure water.

Even if we have sinned, we have confidence to come into the very presence of the Lord, not because of anything we can do, but because of the blood of Jesus. All of our confidence is in Him, not ourselves, and not even in our ability to repent. Even so, this gives us an even greater confidence to draw close to God. Remember that He loved us enough to send us His Son to make the atonement for our sins. The atonement of the cross is enough for even the greatest of sins. His atonement not only reconciles us to God, but is also great enough to cleanse our consciences and make us pure. Therefore, never let your sins or shortcomings drive you away from the Lord, but rather to Him. Stay at the cross until you are intimate with Him again.

DAY 39

The Exile

Then the LORD God said, "Behold, the man has become like one of Us, knowing good and evil; and now, lest he stretch out his hand, and take also from the tree of life, and eat, and live forever"—

therefore the LORD God sent him out from the garden of Eden, to cultivate the ground from which he was taken.

So He drove the man out; and at the east of the garden of Eden He stationed the cherubim, and the flaming sword which turned every direction, to guard the way to the tree of life (Genesis 3:22-24).

This is the tragedy of disobedience. Man was created for fellowship with God, and that fellowship was broken. The garden was created for man, and was to be his perfect home, but after the fall he could no longer stay. When discord entered into our relationship to God, we were also cast into discord with the rest of His creation. Man now dwells in a place of continual strife. As we are redeemed, and our relationships to God is restored, we are also restored to a place of harmony with His creation. This is a part of the gospel, and it is part of the message we have been given to carry. As He said in Mark 16:15, **And He said to them, "Go into all the world and preach the gospel to all creation."** Paradise will be restored as we see in Romans 8:19-22:

For the anxious longing of the creation waits eagerly for the revealing of the sons of God.

For the creation was subjected to futility, not of its own will, but because of Him who subjected it, in hope

that the creation itself also will be set free from its slavery to corruption into the freedom of the glory of the children of God.

For we know that the whole creation groans and suffers the pains of childbirth together until now.

Even so, there is relatively little said about the restoration of the creation in Scripture, because that is obviously for the age to come. Before we can be used to accomplish the restoration, we must have our relationships to God fully restored, and then our relationships to our fellow men. This restoration of fellowship between men actually begins with the restoration of the intended relationship between men and women.

As we review the curses that came upon the man and the woman because of the fall, we see that the struggle of the woman would be in bringing forth her family. The struggle of the man would be with his work. In general, the great gifts that women have been given are relational. In general, the primary gifts men have been given are in regard to their work. Women tend to be people oriented, and men tend to be task oriented. This needs to be understood so we can relate to one another, and become the teams that we were created to be.

These are generalizations about men and women, and generalizations are seldom always true. Almost all men are to some degree relational, and people oriented, and some may be even more so than some women. Almost all women are also to some degree task oriented, and some are even more so than many men. Even so, generally, women are more relational, and men are more task oriented because God made us this way. Therefore, it takes a marriage of both gifts for the ultimate accomplishments in life.

Without this marriage, we will tend to have many great things built or accomplished that no one needs, or wants. Or we can have great relationships that do not accomplish anything. For this reason, many of the great ministries and churches that are raised up strictly by the leadership of men may be huge and expansive, but fail to really build the family of God. The church is called to be a family first, not an organization. When we cease to be a family to just become an organization, we have ceased to be the church. However, if we go to the other extreme, we can have a great big family that does not accomplish anything for the kingdom.

The whole tenor of Scripture reveals that God is a family man, and building His family is fundamental to what He is doing in the earth. He is repeatedly referred to as our Father, and we are His children. However, there can be no Father, or children, without a mother. Paul lamented in I Corinthians 4:15: **"For if you were to have countless tutors in Christ, yet you would not have many fathers."**

A father is not just someone who leads, but someone who reproduces. There are many great teachers and preachers in the church today, but not many are reproducing themselves and releasing other ministries. For someone to be a father, a woman must be present, and this will continue until women are given their proper place in the building and leadership of the church. If they are not given this, we will continue to be project oriented rather than becoming the family that we are called to be. However, if the relational side of our makeup tends to dominate the leadership of a church or ministry without the proper balance of the task oriented part, we will tend to be a big happy place, but not accomplish much. We need both.

DAY 40

The Offering

> Now the man had relations with his wife Eve, and she conceived and gave birth to Cain, and she said, "I have gotten a manchild with the help of the LORD."
>
> And again, she gave birth to his brother Abel. And Abel was a keeper of flocks, but Cain was a tiller of the ground.
>
> So it came about in the course of time that Cain brought an offering to the LORD of the fruit of the ground.
>
> And Abel, on his part also brought of the firstlings of his flock and of their fat portions. And the LORD had regard for Abel and for his offering;
>
> but for Cain and for his offering He had no regard. So Cain became very angry and his countenance fell (Genesis 4:1-5).

The first two sons born to the man and woman had a striking difference in their natures. Just as the Lord made men and women different, He created every individual to be unique. He obviously loves creativity, but this leads us to one of those ultimate questions. Why does the church, which represents God to the world, tend to be so boringly uniform? Why is the church, which is supposed to be one with the Creator, tend to be so void of creativity, prone to follow the trends of the world, and usually only limping along years behind it? Those who know the Creator should be the most creative people on the face of the earth. We must cast off the oppressive yokes of limited vision imposed by counterfeit spiritual authorities that pressure the church into conformity. The church is going to be free. Then she will astonish the world with her creativity, and instead of following the trends of the world, the world will start following her.

The struggle for freedom began among the first two brothers. Jealousy led to oppression. Jealousy is always rooted in insecurity, and it has continually been the source of most human conflicts. We see in Matthew 27:18 and Mark 15:10 that it was because of jealousy that the Lord was delivered to be crucified. We also see repeatedly in the book of Acts, and the apostolic epistles, that persecution was often motivated by jealousy.

We are told in James 3:16, **"For where jealousy and selfish ambition exist, there is disorder and every evil thing."** The true root of almost every division within the church is jealousy. Men may use differences in doctrines and other things as excuses, but at the root of them will usually be jealousy. It is the root of almost every human conflict, and is the source of the stifling oppression that seeks to crush uniqueness and creativity. We must learn to recognize and repent of this evil in our own lives, and resist the influence it seeks to impose on us through others.

The root of jealousy that was manifested in Cain can be traced to his occupation. Cain was a tiller of the ground, which speaks of earthly mindedness. The ground had been cursed so that it would only bear fruit by sweat, which speaks of human effort, or our own works. This is fine for farmers, but Cain tried to offer the fruit of his own works to the Lord, which will never be an acceptable offering to Him. As Paul said in Acts 17:25, **"neither is He served by human hands."**

Abel offered a blood sacrifice, which God accepted. This was a prophecy of the blood sacrifice of Jesus that would alone be an acceptable offering to God. That the sacrifice was offered by the younger son, was also a prophecy that it would be the "last Adam" that would make the sacrifice acceptable to God. From the very beginning, the Lord made a provision for the redemption of the fallen world, and also from the very beginning, prophetic actions point us to Jesus and the redemption of the cross.

The acceptance of Abel's sacrifice and the rejection of his own, outraged Cain. This was a prophecy of the enmity that would exist between those who tried to offer God their own good works for acceptance, and those who would trust in the blood of Jesus. Jesus was not persecuted by the base sinners of society, but rather the self-righteous. The same is still true. There are many, including some who claim to be Christians, that put their trust in their own works as their righteousness. They usually try to make the New Testament into another law, the fruit of the Tree of the Knowledge of Good and Evil. They will likewise rage against and persecute those who base their faith on the righteousness of the cross. Therefore, seen in the first two sons is the nature of the serpent, and the nature of the one who would defeat the serpent by His death. Trust in the cross. It will bring persecution for a time, but it has already gained the ultimate victory.

DAY 41

Sin and Depression

Then the LORD said to Cain, "Why are you angry? And why has your countenance fallen?
"If you do well, will not your countenance be lifted up? And if you do not do well, sin is crouching at the door; and its desire is for you, but you must master it" (Genesis 4:6- 7).

For one's "countenance to fall" is used biblically to describe depression. Depression is the tendency to see things from a dark or gloomy perspective. This problem is growing dramatically in our times. It is consistently found as a root problem of those who commit serious violent crimes and mass murders. As we will see in this chapter, it also led to Cain killing his brother Abel.

Those who suffer from depression are not all potential murderers. Most people deal with this problem in a nonaggressive, internal way. However, for those who turn inward, it leads to the destruction of their own personality, and in the more extreme cases, suicide.

God gives the remedy to depression in the above verses. It is so simple that most cannot accept it. Some, including many schools of psychology, would even say that it was the Lord's rejection of Cain that led to his depression, but that is the superficial understanding of the problem. If the Lord had accepted Cain's offering, it would have hardened him in his self-righteousness. The Lord had to reject his sacrifice to correct Cain's perspective in a way that could lead to his salvation.

Rejection is always hard to take, but it is good for us and needful if we are doing something wrong. Rejection is a factor that can lead to the greatest breakthroughs in our lives. It is hard to find a single person in history who accomplished anything of significance who did not suffer a major rejection or failure in their lives. Rejection will either make us bitter or better, which is basically what the Lord said to Cain.

As the Lord explained to Cain, the way to be delivered from our depression is not by having someone accept us the way we are, but by someone loving us enough to correct us so that we can do what is right.

With the exception of chemically induced depression, it will almost always be the result of us doing something wrong, or by failing to do what we know is right. The way out of the depression is what the Lord told Cain—start doing what is right.

Modern psychology and psychoanalysis have tried to relieve people from depression by attacking moral standards which they believe are unrealistic for people to try to live by. This is a basic attempt to change what we believe to be right and wrong. In some ways, this is understandable because religious men and women have often added to God's Word, and imposed a legalism that is destructive to the human personality. However, sin is sin and we can say that it is not sin, but the Lord placed a conscience in us that knows intuitively that it is. The more we try to rationalize it, the more depression will take root in our lives, just as Cain was warned. The only way out of this depression is to repent of the sin and start doing what is right.

It is noteworthy that the Lord did not tell Cain to stop doing what is wrong, but to simply "do right." Legalists will focus on getting people to stop doing what is wrong, but the Lord emphasized the positive, doing what is right. As Jesus taught us, loving God and our neighbors is the fulfillment of the Law. In this way, the positives that we do through love will automatically keep us from doing what is wrong. For example, if we love God, we will not worship idols. If we love our neighbors, we will not steal from them, envy what is theirs, or murder them. The simple way out of depression is to start doing what is right, in love.

Depression and the resulting suicide and murder is becoming epidemic among today's youth. It is interesting that these problems seem to have not even existed before the child labor laws were instituted. Certainly there was a need to protect children from the abuses some suffered during those times. However, these laws went to an extreme that actually released even more serious problems upon the youth. They destroyed the important institutions of apprenticeship that enabled children to learn responsibility and engage in meaningful employment during the years when they most need focus, purpose, and responsibility. As the proverb states, "Idleness is the devil's workshop," and he has certainly used the idleness of youth that was forced upon them with these laws. Therefore, we must redouble our efforts as parents to give our children meaningful duties and responsibilities, especially during puberty. What is now their worst years can be their best years if they learn to "do right." If they are positively employed, depression will seldom find a door into their lives.

DAY 42

Jealousy and Murder

And Cain told Abel his brother. And it came about when they were in the field, that Cain rose up against Abel his brother and killed him (Genesis 4:8).

When there were just two brothers on the earth, they could not get along. When there were just two cars registered in the state of New Jersey, they had a collision! We have a problem getting along. The transgression that robbed mankind of everlasting life quickly led to the taking of life, murder. Man had taken on the nature of the evil one they had listened to in the garden. As the Lord said in John 8:44, when He was chastising the Pharisees:

"You are of your father the devil, and you want to do the desires of your father. He was a murderer from the beginning, and does not stand in the truth, because there is no truth in him. Whenever he speaks a lie, he speaks from his own nature; for he is a liar, and the father of lies."

Satan's purpose on earth is to kill and destroy. He does this through lies. We are told in I John 3:8: **"The Son of God appeared for this purpose, that He might destroy the works of the devil."** The Lord came to destroy lies and murder by giving life and revealing the truth. The Lord prayed in John 17:18: **"As Thou didst send Me into the world, I also have sent them into the world."** It is likewise our purpose while on the earth to destroy these works of the devil by walking in the life and light of the Lord. The Lord promised in Matthew 16:18, that the gates of hell would not prevail against His church. The life that is in Christ is more powerful than death. The truth that is in Christ is more powerful than any lie. Life and truth will ultimately prevail.

To understand how life and truth will prevail, we must understand the **"gates of hell" (Matthew 16:18).** Gates are doors, or access points. The gates of hell are doors that hell is using to gain entrance into the world, the church, and even our own lives. The original gate of hell was in the garden. He gained access to the world by convincing the man and woman, who had been given authority over the world, to believe his lies. Once man listened to the devil, because the devil was **"a murderer from the beginning" (John 8:44),** it was inevitable for man to become a murderer. The lie that he used to lead to the release of murder was envy, or jealousy.

Cain allowed the jealousy he felt toward his brother's acceptance by the Lord to drive him to an even worse sin, murder. Jealousy, or envy, is still found as a root cause of murder in the world. We are even told that Jesus was crucified because of envy (see Matthew 27:18; Mark 15:10), and the persecutions that rose against the apostles and early church were because of jealousy (see Acts 5:17; 13:45).

How will the church be used to shut this door of hell which can lead even to murder? First, we will not have authority over the devil in others if he has a root in our own lives. Jealousy can ultimately lead to murder, but it is also the root of many seemingly lesser, but destructive sins. As we read before in James 3:16, jealousy is usually linked to selfish ambition. The result will be disorder, or division, and can be the opening to **"every evil thing."**

Jealousy is almost always found to be the true root of divisions within the body of Christ today. Men will usually try to justify their actions by claiming that their reasons are something else, but the real root is usually jealousy. It can rise in the heart of any of us. If it does and we do not repent of it, jealousy can destroy the work of Christ, or will at least do it damage. Even so, in the end the church will prevail against this terrible gate of hell. How? Love is the truth that will ultimately overcome jealousy. We are told in I Corinthians 13:4-8:

> **Love is patient, love is kind, and is not jealous; love does not brag and is not arrogant,**
>
> **does not act unbecomingly; it does not seek its own, is not provoked, does not take into account a wrong suffered,**
>
> **does not rejoice in unrighteousness, but rejoices with the truth;**
>
> **bears all things, believes all things, hopes all things, endures all things.**
>
> **Love never fails**.

Jealousy divided the first two brothers, but love will ultimately unite those who are in Christ, so no evil will be able to stand against them. We are told that "the gates of hell will not prevail against the church," singular (see Matthew 16:18). When we are united, the gates of hell cannot prevail against us. When we are divided, they will. But love will ultimately prevail, and before the end there will be a church that stands together in unity because they love one another. Let us determine in our hearts right now that we are going to be controlled by love, not envy. If we do this we cannot fail because **"Love never fails."**

DAY 43

The Curse from the Ground

> Then the LORD said to Cain, "Where is Abel your brother?" And he said, "I do not know. Am I my brother's keeper?"
>
> And He said, "What have you done? The voice of your brother's blood is crying to Me from the ground.
>
> "And now you are cursed from the ground, which has opened its mouth to receive your brother's blood from your hand.
>
> "When you cultivate the ground, it shall no longer yield its strength to you; you shall be a vagrant and a wanderer on the earth" (Genesis 4:9-12).

Curses release the powers of evil against us. Because the devil was **"a murderer from the beginning" (John 8:44),** few things can release his evil powers like the shedding of innocent blood. Here we see that Cain was **"cursed from the ground"** because he murdered his brother. The very earth itself curses man today in many regions because of the innocent blood that has been shed upon it. Therefore, many revivals and moves of God could not be released in these regions until there was repentance for the sins that had been committed in those places by previous generations.

Why would the curse brought on by one generation, get passed on to the next? Because every time there is sin, there is a wound that is inflicted upon the glorious harmony that was originally established in the creation. For wounds to be healed they must be disinfected and closed, which is true throughout the creation. For the consequences of sin to be removed, there must be repentance, reconciliation, and restoration. A good biblical example of this is found in II Samuel 21:1:

> Now there was a famine in the days of David for three years, year after year; and David sought the presence of the LORD. And the LORD said, "It is for Saul and his bloody house, because he put the Gibeonites to death."

King David's administration suffered a famine for a sin that his predecessor had committed. The curse did not come upon David's administration to punish him, but because the ground was cursed. When the curse became evident, David made restitution to those who had been wounded by Saul's sin so that the curse could be removed. Thus, we find righteous men in Scripture such as Daniel and Nehemiah asking forgiveness for the sins of their fathers. The reason that the sins of the fathers are passed on to following generations is not to punish the children for what the previous generations did, but to remove the curse and bring repentance and restoration. Curses upon regions are to alert the righteous that the healing of a spiritual wound in that region is needed.

King David lived under the law, so the only way the curse could be removed because of Saul's sin was to let the Gibeonites have revenge on Saul's house. Under the law it was an **"eye for an eye and a tooth for a tooth" (Exodus 21:24).** However, we are no longer under the law. The curse is now removed by the cross of Jesus.

Even so, there must be an acknowledgment of sin, and repentance for the cross to be applied. For there to be repentance, there must be an identification with the sinner, or credentials for repentance. It required the King of Israel to repent for the sins of the previous king. Likewise, only a white man can repent of the sins of white men against blacks. Only a Baptist could repent for the sins of the Baptists, or a Charismatic for the sins of the Charismatics.

"Reconciliation" movements have arisen in the church in recent years to do just this. They have resulted in extraordinary releases of God's grace on cities, countries, and even whole regions of the world. Repentance for social and spiritual sins committed in our history is not the only thing that is needed to release revival, but it can sometimes be the spark that brings the release of life and light. Our personal repentance can do the same in our personal lives. This can also be true for a church. Many churches suffer under an unnecessary curse because they have not repented for previous sins that they committed as a church, or even the sins of previous leaders of the church.

In the text from Genesis about Cain, the curse from the ground caused him to become a wanderer on the earth. Because man was created to cultivate the earth, the earth needs man. However, we can never be completely at home, or at peace with the earth, until the curses have been removed that are the result of human sins against one another. This is why the problems with refugees, such as the Jews and the Palestinians, are problems that can threaten the peace of the whole world. The reason that regions cannot seem to free themselves from poverty, can often be traced to the sins of previous generations. In all things, repentance can be the beginning of the release of God's grace and favor in our lives.

DAY 44

Departing from the Lord

> And Cain said to the LORD, "My punishment is too great to bear!
>
> "Behold, Thou hast driven me this day from the face of the ground; and from Thy face I shall be hidden, and I shall be a vagrant and a wanderer on the earth, and it will come about that whoever finds me will kill me."
>
> So the LORD said to him, "Therefore whoever kills Cain, vengeance will be taken on
>
> him sevenfold." And the LORD appointed a sign for Cain, lest anyone finding him should slay him.
>
> Then Cain went out from the presence of the LORD, and settled in the land of Nod, east of Eden (Genesis 4:13-16).

When the Lord told Cain how he could be delivered from depression he did not listen. When we do not heed the Lord, it will usually result in our falling even further into sin, just as it did with Cain. Cain still could have turned to the Lord, humbled himself and repented, and he would have received help. The Lord warned him that he had to master the sin, but he continued down the path of letting his sin master him.

It is interesting that, even then, Cain understood the law of sowing and reaping, which Paul explained in Galatians 6:7: **"Do not be deceived, God is not mocked; for whatever a man sows, this he will also reap."** He knew that because he had murdered his brother that he was in danger of being murdered himself. This is a law that is as sure as the law of gravity. Therefore, if we want to receive grace, we should learn to sow grace every chance that we get. If we want to receive mercy, we should learn to sow mercy every chance we get. If we do good, we will reap good. If we do evil, we will reap the same.

When reading about Cain's fear of being murdered, one might think, "Who is going to murder him?" Adam and Eve lived nearly one thousand years. They did begin to fulfill their commission to multiply and fill the earth, having many other sons and daughters. Obviously, there was already a population on the earth by the time Cain slew Abel. They were obviously close relatives to Cain, but he was still afraid of them. He had slain his own brother, so he knew that a brother could slay him. This was accurate enough, because all men ultimately derive their name from the same family, but that has never kept them from attacking one another.

Even so, the Lord had mercy on Cain. He gave him a mark that would serve to protect him. Throughout the history of God's dealings with mankind, He has been quick to show unmerited grace and mercy to us. His grace and mercy is even enough for Him to negate the law of sowing and reaping. Throughout the Scriptures, we have many examples of the Lord causing crop failures from the evil seeds men have sown. However, we also have examples of swift judgment for those who have hardened their hearts and presumed upon His grace and mercy.

The worst result of Cain's sin of murdering his brother was that he **"went out from the presence of the Lord."** When fighting occurs between brethren in churches, or between churches, this is often the ultimate result. Many will end up actually departing from the Lord. That is why, from the very beginning, one of the enemy's primary strategies is to get brothers to fight with each other. He is called **"the accuser of our brethren" (Revelation 12:10),** because one of his most effective weapons against us is to get us accusing one another.

Cain somehow thought that Abel was the reason for his rejection. The rejection of Cain's offering had nothing to do with Abel's offering. The answer to Cain's problem had nothing to do with Abel, but with himself. However, from the beginning, blaming someone else for our own problems has been one of the primary deceptions that has kept men from the grace of God. It has also led to the most destructive wars in history, and it has led to the most destructive wars between churches in history.

First, the enemy will try to get us to be jealous of others. Then he will get us to accuse them of being the reason for our own problems. That is why nations that are having serious difficulties become so dangerous. It often seems much easier to blame someone else and attack them instead of dealing with our own problems. People will tend to rally around us if we can portray a common enemy that is causing our problems. Churches, and people, can become dangerous when they start having serious problems. If you see them starting to attack and blame others, it is time to depart. We must not continue to get caught in this trap of the enemy, which is the seemingly cheap escape from dealing with our own shortcomings. It will lead us to needlessly wounding others. Even worse than that, it will also lead us to **"departing from the presence of the Lord."**

DAY 45

They Called Upon the Lord

And Adam had relations with his wife again; and she gave birth to a son, and named him Seth, for, she said, "God has appointed me another offspring in place of Abel; for Cain killed him."

And to Seth, to him also a son was born; and he called his name Enosh. Then men began to call upon the name of the LORD (Genesis 4:25-26).

After the original transgression in the garden, the corruption of mankind continued on a downward spiral. The Lord created man to be free, and He would let man go his own way. Yet, in His unfathomable compassion, He continued to bless them and help them as much as He could. The Lord knew the end from the beginning, and from the beginning He planned and prepared for man's ultimate redemption and restoration from his sin.

All of God's ways are so much higher than man's that we will be spending eternity learning about Him. He stretched out the galaxies like a curtain, with billions upon billions of stars in each one. He set the earth in such a tiny slice of orbit that if we deviated just the equivalent of one-eighth of an inch over a one hundred-mile distance we would either freeze or fry. He set the earth on a tilting axis so that the seasons would change, alternately melting the ice so that it would not wobble out of its orbit. Then He set the moon and other planets in their appointed orbits so that their gravitational pulls would perfectly stabilize the earth. If any of these things changed, the earth would quickly drift out of its orbit and all life would perish. Scientists have conceded that if the power of all of the computers in the world were added together, they could not compute the odds that all of this just happened by accident. When we begin adding the extraordinary balance of nature needed on the planet to sustain life, we know that the mind of God is far, far beyond our ability to comprehend. When we look at the heavens, the whole earth is but a speck of dust, like a single grain of sand to the oceans. King David wondered:

When I consider Thy heavens, the work of Thy fingers, the moon and the stars, which Thou hast ordained;
What is man, that Thou dost take thought of him? And the son of man, that Thou dost care for him? (Psalm 8:3-4).

God not only considers man, but He has chosen to dwell with man. For some incomprehensible reason, He loves us. He even loved us enough to empty Himself and become one of us for our salvation. As much as He can without violating the freedom that He gave us, He fixes our mistakes and blesses us even though most of the time we do not even know it. Eve may have been deceived by the serpent, but she realized that it was the Lord who gave her another son.

After Enosh was born, we are told that it was then men began to call upon the name of the Lord. The Hebrew word for "call" that is used here is *qara,* which indicates more than just calling out to Him. It also implies that they began "proclaiming," or "acknowledging," the Lord. This is the beginning of our return to the light. To not see God in creation is a profound delusion, a darkness so deep that it is an intellectual black hole. A black hole is a term used for anomalies in space that have such a gravitational pull that even light cannot escape them. Men have in our times fallen into such intellectual depravity that they cannot acknowledge God, even though the scientific evidence that He exists is so overwhelming. Even so, from the beginning, there has always been some who would proclaim Him.

Man can fall into the deepest depravity, but if he still has enough light to call upon the name of the Lord, he can be saved. The incomprehensible love of God will not reject anyone who turns to Him, just as we are promised in Acts 2:21: **"And it shall be, that everyone who calls on the name of the Lord shall be saved."** This is repeated and elaborated on in Romans 10:12-14:

> **...the same Lord is Lord of all, abounding in riches for all who call upon Him;**
> **for "Whoever will call upon the name of the Lord will be saved."**
> **How then shall they call upon Him in whom they have not believed? And how shall they believe in Him whom they have not heard? And how shall they hear without a preacher?**

The Lord is **"abounding in riches for all who call upon Him."** These are the true riches of the kingdom—the truth and the knowledge of God's ways. We are also told that others cannot believe without a preacher. How can we who have been blessed with such great riches not proclaim Him? To **"call upon the name of the Lord"** is more than just praying to Him, it is also to proclaim Him. How can we not share in the unlimited wealth that comes from the knowledge of His ways, if we have been touched by His love?

DAY 46

Walking With God

Then Jared lived eight hundred years after he became the father of Enoch...And Enoch lived sixty-five years, and became the father of Methuselah.

Then Enoch walked with God three hundred years after he became the father of Methuselah, and he had other sons and daughters.

So all the days of Enoch were three hundred and sixty-five years.

And Enoch walked with God; and he was not, for God took him (Genesis 5:19, 21-24).

Enoch is one of the most remarkable, and inspirational characters in the Bible. He walked with God in such a way that he did not have to taste death because God just took him. We read in Hebrews 11:5:

By faith Enoch was taken up so that he should not see death; and he was not found because God took him up; for he obtained the witness that before his being taken up he was pleasing to God.

Adam was still alive during Enoch's days. It is probable that Enoch talked with Adam about what it was like to have walked with God before the fall. Something must have stirred within him, a desire to have that same kind of intimate relationship to God that Adam once had, and he pursued it. God responded.

No where does it say in Scripture that Enoch is the only one who can do this. In fact, we are promised in James 4:8 that if we, **"Draw near to God and He will draw near to you."** We are all as close to God as we want to be. The veil has been rent and we can all enter into the presence of the Lord by the blood of Jesus. We can be as close to God as anyone in the Scriptures has been. This is not a presumption, because the Scriptures are full of invitations for us to draw near to Him. He created us for that purpose, to have fellowship with Him. If there is anything that can measure the degree to which redemption has worked in our lives, it would be how close we are to Him. The only thing that prevents us from being as close to God as Enoch is our own desire.

Our God is an awesome, holy God. He is a consuming fire, and when we get close to Him the wood, hay, and stubble in our lives will burn. Even so, we do not have to wait until we are perfect to draw near to God, but it is by drawing near to Him that we are changed, as we read in Hebrews 4:15-16:

For we do not have a high priest who cannot sympathize with our weaknesses, but One who has been tempted in all things as we are, yet without sin.
Let us therefore draw near with confidence to the throne of grace, that we may receive mercy and may find grace to help in time of need.

If we sin and fall short of the grace of God, we must learn to run to Him, not away from Him as Adam and Eve did. We can never hide from Him anyway, but He has also proven throughout the Scriptures that He will not force us to come close to Him. We have to want to be close enough to Him to seek Him. He promised in Jeremiah 29:13: **"And you will seek Me and find Me, when you search for Me with all your heart."** If we are going to be that close to Him, we must desire Him enough to sacrifice all of the things that would distract us. We must choose to draw near to Him when we could be doing other things.

We have another very interesting statement about Enoch in Jude 14, **"And about these also Enoch, in the seventh generation from Adam, prophesied, saying, "Behold, the Lord came with many thousands of His holy ones."** Enoch is the very first one recorded in Scripture who prophesied. This reveals the true essence and foundation of an authentic prophetic ministry, which is simply to get so close to God that you are His friend. Friends share their plans and purposes with each other. That is why the Lord said in Amos 3:7: **"Surely the Lord GOD does nothing unless He reveals His secret counsel to His servants the prophets."**

Nowhere has the Lord obligated Himself to do anything without first revealing it to His prophets. He does this because He wants to. He wants to because the prophets are His friends. There is nothing that prevents us from being that close to God. There is nothing that says that we cannot walk with God to the point that He just takes us up like He did Enoch. Could this in fact be what the rapture really is?

DAY 47

Noah and the Nephilim

Now it came about, when men began to multiply on the face of the land, and daughters were born to them,

that the sons of God saw that the daughters of men were beautiful; and they took wives for themselves, whomever they chose.

Then the LORD said, "My Spirit shall not strive with man forever, because he also is flesh; nevertheless his days shall be one hundred and twenty years."

The Nephilim were on the earth in those days, and also afterward, when the sons of God came in to the daughters of men, and they bore children to them. Those were the mighty men who were of old, men of renown (Genesis 6:1-4).

It is obvious in Scripture that angels have the ability to take on the form of men. It was for this reason that we are told in Hebrews 13:2, **"Do not neglect to show hospitality to strangers, for by this some have entertained angels without knowing it."** Angels are ministering spirits who serve the heirs of salvation (see Hebrews 1:14). They love God, and God loves them. We must learn to be comfortable in the presence of angels because there is a great deal of interchange between them and mankind, especially believers. We must also know the limits of their relationship to mankind, and to be able to distinguish the fallen angels from those who have kept their estate and continue to serve God.

In the scripture quoted above, we see that some angels (which are sometimes called **"the sons of God"** in Scripture), left their estate to join themselves to women who bore them children. This brought forth a race of super men that God did not create called the Nephilim. Many theologians believe that these were the basis for gods of Greek mythology, and other ancient legends. This super race brought forth a corruption and violence that the earth could not stand, and they, therefore, had to be destroyed.

125

> Then the LORD saw that the wickedness of man was great on the earth, and that every intent of the thoughts of his heart was only evil continually.
>
> And the LORD was sorry that He had made man on the earth, and He was grieved in His heart.
>
> And the LORD said, "I will blot out man whom I have created from the face of the land, from man to animals to creeping things and to birds of the sky; for I am sorry that I have made them."
>
> But Noah found favor in the eyes of the LORD.
>
> These are the records of the generations of Noah. Noah was a righteous man, blameless in his time; Noah walked with God (Genesis 6:5-9).

The Hebrew word that is translated **"blameless"** in verse 9 is *tamiym* (taw-meem'), which literally means "having integrity, truth, without blemish, complete, full, perfect, sound, undefiled, etc." We are told that Noah was a **"righteous man"** concerning his character, but **"blameless in his time"** is also translated "perfect in his generations." This had to do with his genealogy. It is a reference to him not having the mixture that came from the fallen angels. That is why the generations of Noah are so important here. He was still a pure man, not having the mixture brought through the fallen angels.

God created man perfectly for his purpose on the earth. Man was created to have fellowship with God who is Spirit. Therefore, mankind will always have a spiritual yearning for fellowship with God. It is also clear that the Lord, knowing the end from the beginning, always intended to bring forth the new creation man through His Son. The new creation is far superior to the original creation because the new creation man is empowered with supernatural gifts and power. The Scriptures are clear that some will not only do the works that Jesus did, but greater works, as we read in John 14:12-13:

> "Truly, truly, I say to you, he who believes in Me, the works that I do shall he do also; and greater works than these shall he do; because I go to the Father.
>
> "And whatever you ask in My name, that will I do, that the Father may be glorified in the Son.

Christians who are born again by the Spirit of God are in fact a "super race." However, this is not the result of a carnal mixture of flesh and spirit. The Nephilim were Satan's attempt to preempt the new creation, which the Lord was going to bring forth by giving His Spirit to men. When the church becomes all that it is called to be, believers will be considered **"men of renown,"** because of the great works that they do. However, these will be works of righteousness, not violence. They will be done in love to heal and restore, in obedience to the Holy Spirit who is holy in all of His works

DAY 48

The Judgment

Then God said to Noah, "The end of all flesh has come before Me; for the earth is filled with violence because of them; and behold, I am about to destroy them with the earth.

"Make for yourself an ark...

"And behold, I, even I am bringing the flood of water upon the earth, to destroy all flesh...

"But I will establish My covenant with you; and you shall enter the ark—you and your sons and your wife, and your sons' wives with you.

"And of every living thing of all flesh, you shall bring two of every kind into the ark, to keep them alive with you...

Thus Noah did; according to all that God had commanded him, so he did (Genesis 6:13-14, 17-19, 22).

The Lord's patience is beyond comprehension. In Revelation 2:20-21, we see that the Lord even gave Jezebel **"time to repent."** However, the very patience of the Lord is in itself a type of judgment. As Ecclesiastes 8:11 says, **"Because the sentence against an evil deed is not executed quickly, therefore the hearts of the sons of men among them are given fully to do evil."** The wicked will interpret the delay of God's discipline as evidence that He does not really care about the evil they do. Therefore, they will fall into increasing depravity. Only the truly righteous, or those who have righteousness in their hearts, will understand that His patience is indeed His grace.

His patience is there so we can repent. As we are told in I Corinthians 11:31, **"But if we judged ourselves rightly, we should not be judged."** As the Lord said in Matthew 21:44, **"And he who falls on this stone will be broken to pieces; but on whomever it falls, it will scatter him like dust."** It is better to fall on the rock and be broken than to have it fall on us. It is better to humble ourselves and repent than to have Him judge us.

The Lord will give us time to repent and discipline ourselves so that He does not have to do it. Even so, the patience of the Lord does have its limit. There is a point when He will bring swift judgment to our sin. It is a tragic mistake to ever presume upon His grace because for a time we were able to get away with something.

The Lord beheld the corruption that was on the earth and He determined to wipe out all living flesh and begin again with a remnant that He preserved. This is a precedent that we see repeated at times in the Scripture, and in history. Mankind had a great calling, to be the habitation of the Lord Himself, and Satan was able to corrupt and pervert this calling, forcing God to destroy men whom He had created. However, there has always been a remnant that Satan was unable to corrupt, who the Lord could use to continue moving men toward His ultimate purpose.

There are many individuals, families, churches, and movements that have had a high calling which the enemy has likewise been able to corrupt. The Lord Himself has had to remove many whom He called. Even so, there is usually a remnant that He can use as seed to continue His purposes in another place or time. For this reason, many of the greatest leaders who accomplish great advances for the kingdom have come out of previous movements or churches that have failed.

Many who experience the terrible disappointment of church splits or failures, allow this to neutralize them so that they are never effectively used again for the kingdom. Others build an ark by which they are able to rise above the flood of judgment, preserving a remnant for the future accomplishment of their purposes.

As stated, everything that has happened to us was allowed by God for our maturity. These things will either make us bitter or make us better. Christ is the Ark into which we may enter to rise above any situations or problems that come upon the earth. If we abide in Him, there is no flood that can overcome us. In Him, there is a peace that no storm can penetrate. He is the Fortress that no enemy can ever conquer. When we are confronted by situations where we know that destruction is coming, do not just run from the situation, but run into the Ark.

If we are abiding in Christ, we are abiding in His Spirit. His Spirit is manifested by **"love, joy, peace, patience, kindness, goodness, faithfulness, gentleness, self-control..." (Galatians 5:22-23).** When we are fully abiding in Him, nothing can penetrate this fruit in our lives. No onslaught will cause us to stop loving, stop having the joy of the Lord, stop having patience with those who assail us, stop showing kindness, goodness, being faithful, gentle, and self-controlled. The attacks of the enemy are intended to make us compromise the fruit of the Spirit, which is to get us out of our place of abiding in the Ark, so that we will also go down with the flood.

DAY 49

The Covenant

"And the LORD said to Himself, "I will never again curse the ground on account of man, for the intent of man's heart is evil from his youth; and I will never again destroy every living thing, as I have done.

"While the earth remains, seedtime and harvest, and cold and heat, and summer and winter, and day and night shall not cease."

Then God spoke to Noah and to his sons with him, saying,

"Now behold, I Myself do establish My covenant with you, and with your descendants after you;

and with every living creature that is with you, the birds, the cattle, and every beast of the earth with you; of all that comes out of the ark, even every beast of the earth.

"And I establish My covenant with you; and all flesh shall never again be cut off by the water of the flood, neither shall there again be a flood to destroy the earth."

And God said, "This is the sign of the covenant which I am making between Me and you and every living creature that is with you, for all successive generations;

I set My bow in the cloud, and it shall be for a sign of a covenant between Me and the earth (Genesis 8:21-22; 9:8-13).

Because the hearts of men had become fully given to do evil, judgment was necessary. Even so, through judgment He gave the earth a new beginning. From time to time, He would have to judge cities, regions, or cultures, but here He made His first covenant with man: He would not curse the ground further, and He would not destroy the whole earth again with a flood. He then set as the sign of the covenant a rainbow in the clouds. From this time, whenever rain is mentioned in Scripture, it refers to blessing.

Why would the Almighty God make a covenant with fallen man? Whenever two make a covenant, both will usually have something to contribute. If the covenant is one sided, it is because the strongest party in the agreement can dominate the weaker. Almighty God does not need anything from man, yet repeatedly gives man agreements that are very one sided in man's favor. One of the great problems of faith has been man's inability to believe that such agreements could possibly be true. Man can offer to God nothing in return except obedience, but that is all that the Lord wants. Death and evil came upon the world because of man's disobedience. Obedience could also restore the earth as we read in Romans 5:19:

> **For as through the one man's disobedience the many were made sinners, even so through the obedience of the One the many will be made righteous.**

God Almighty repeatedly gave His Word to man, and His Word has never failed. He would later make covenants with Abraham, Israel, and then with all who would trust in the cross. His Word is His bond, and He remains faithful. All that He requires of us in return is that we obey Him. Yet, even this is for our sake, for our salvation.

The New Covenant provision is made not only for the complete restoration of man from the consequences of the fall, but through it man is even elevated to a condition higher than man had before the fall. The new creation man does not just walk with God, but we have God living in us. This is beyond the comprehension of even the angels. The Lord not only gives those who will obey Him eternal life, but He even makes them sons and daughters. He even comes to live in them. In return, we have nothing to give Him but love and obedience. Is He not worthy of the devotion and obedience of even every thought that we have?

In Romans 1:5 and 16:26 Paul refers to **"the obedience of faith."** True faith does obey. We enter into the New Covenant by faith in the cross of Jesus. It is not by works, as the Law proved that by our own efforts we can never keep the standard of God's righteousness. Though we may fall short when trying to obey the Law by our own strength, the Lord gives us the grace to obey Him. This grace comes by the Holy Spirit whom He has given to live in us. God not only makes the covenant when we have nothing to offer in return, He also gives us what He expects from us in return. If we love Him enough to want to obey Him, He will give us the provision so that we can walk in obedience. When we agree to this covenant with Him, He gives us all things that are His, making us His own children. For all of eternity, there will never again be a transaction, a deal, or an opportunity, like this one!

Let us show our love and appreciation by obeying the Spirit that He has given to live in us. All that He asks is that we love Him, and love one another. How could we not love the One who is the most glorious, generous, lovable Being there is? How can we not give ourselves fully to pleasing Him in all things?

DAY 50

From Babylon to Abraham

And they said to one another, "Come, let us make bricks and burn them thoroughly." And they used brick for stone, and they used tar for mortar.

And they said, "Come, let us build for ourselves a city, and a tower whose top will reach into heaven, and let us make for ourselves a name; lest we be scattered abroad over the face of the whole earth."

And the LORD came down to see the city and the tower which the sons of men had built.

And the LORD said, "Behold, they are one people, and they all have the same language. And this is what they began to do, and now nothing which they purpose to do will be impossible for them.

"Come, let Us go down and there confuse their language, that they may not understand one another's speech."

So the LORD scattered them abroad from there over the face of the whole earth; and they stopped building the city.

Therefore its name was called Babel, because there the LORD confused the language of the whole earth; and from there the LORD scattered them abroad over the face of the whole earth (Genesis 11:3-9).

In the garden, two seeds were prophesied to come from man. One was the seed of the serpent whose nature was implanted in man when they listened to his voice and obeyed him. The other was the seed that was prophesied to come from the woman that would crush the serpent's head, which was Christ. With the first two sons born, we see the beginning of the nature of each of these seeds. The Bible is the history of the development of these two seeds in men, and God's dealings with them. One brings forth Christ, and the other, when it is fully matured, brings forth the anti-Christ. This story of the Tower of Babel is a profound revelation of the seed that will bring forth the anti-Christ. This is the root of that which becomes "Mystery Babylon" in the book of Revelation.

We tend to think of the serpent only in its most blatantly evil nature. However, the tree whose fruit brings death is the knowledge of both good and evil. The good side of the Tree of Knowledge is just as deadly as the evil side, and far more deceptive. Satan's most deceptive guise is when he comes as **"an angel of light" (II Corinthians 11:14)**, or what could have been translated, "a messenger of truth." Satan has always been able to do more damage to the truth when he works through religious men, which is why the most religious men of the time were the greatest opposers of Christ. However, the true nature of such religious men can usually be discerned as those who tried to build the Tower of Babel.

The goal of these men seems to be a noble one, to build a tower to heaven. However, their nature is revealed by two basic issues. The first is their reason for building the tower. It was not to get closer to God, but to make a name for themselves, and to have a project that men could gather around. The second way that their nature is revealed is their means for building it, which is their own wisdom and strength. This is the continuing presumption that men can gain the heavenly nature by their own wisdom and strength. But as the Lord said in Zechariah 4:6, **"Not by might nor by power, but by My Spirit."**

What the men of Babel vainly sought was what the Lord wants to give to man. He wants us to dwell with Him in the heavenly places, and He wants to gather us together. However, we cannot do it with selfish motives, or our own strength. This may seem like a foolish thing for men to try to do, but it seems that men have not quit trying to build just such a tower. Christians have been just as prone to do it as anyone else. How many of the huge projects that Christians have built, from cathedrals to even some evangelistic outreaches, have been just an attempt by some to make a name for themselves, or to have a project that will gather and motivate men? Many even do these things in an attempt to reach God, or to be acceptable to Him. However, a true ministry does not come in order to reach God, but from a place of having been reached by God through the cross. A true ministry does not come as an attempt to be accepted by Him, but from a position of being accepted by Him through the cross.

The Lord's response to the Tower was to scatter men's languages so that they could not go on building. The result of the project was the opposite of what they were seeking. What are the results of many of the spiritual projects we have tried to devise as Christians? Are they not the same? Now the church is divided into more than 10,000 different denominations and movements, or "languages." It does not matter how much we attach God's name to something, if the motives are rooted in selfish ambition, or an attempt to gather around anything but the Lord Jesus Himself, the ultimate end will only be further division. The only way into heaven, or to gather men, is to be gathered to Christ Jesus Himself. He sits in the heavenly places above all rule and authority and power. If we abide in Him, that is where we, too, will dwell.

After the story of the Tower of Babel we come to Abraham, who was God's antitheses to the folly of Babel.

> **Now the LORD said to Abram, "Go forth from your country, and from your relatives and from your father's house, to the land which I will show you;**
> **And I will make you a great nation, and I will bless you, and make your name great; and so you shall be a blessing;**
> **And I will bless those who bless you, and the one who curses you I will curse. And in you all the families of the earth shall be blessed" (Genesis 12:1-3).**

By faith, Abraham gained the very things that the men of Babel had vainly sought to accomplish by their own strength and wisdom—a name that would be esteemed by every generation, and a place in the city of God that would one day gather all men together again. In the following text from Hebrews 11:8-10, we see how he did this:

> **By faith, Abraham, when he was called, obeyed by going out to a place which he was to receive for an inheritance; and he went out, not knowing where he was going.**
> **By faith, he lived as an alien in the land of promise, as in a foreign land dwelling in tents with Isaac and Jacob, fellow heirs of the same promise;**
> **for he was looking for the city which has foundations, whose architect and builder is God.**

Abraham may not have known where he was going, but he knew what he was looking for. Abraham's faith was demonstrated by the fact that when he was called, he obeyed. In contrast to the men of Babel, Abraham did not build anything. He became very wealthy and could have easily built a city, but he lived in tents all the days of his life. He was not seeking an earthly city, but a heavenly one. He knew that his earthly dwelling was temporary, so he was not overly concerned about living in a tent.

There is a saying that "you can be so heavenly minded that you are not any earthly good." This sounds cute, but the reverse is actually true. If we are too earthly minded, we will not be any good for heaven or the earth. Abraham was an alien and stranger on the earth. The goal of his life was to have a place in what God was building, not men. Because His focus was on God instead of men, he became a blessing to every family on the face of the earth. Those who will likewise give themselves to the eternal purposes of God will accomplish far more for those who are on the earth as well.

In John 8:39 there is an interesting dispute between the Pharisees and Jesus, **They answered and said to Him, "Abraham is our father." Jesus said to them, "If you are Abraham's children, do the deeds of Abraham."** Paul, the apostle, also elaborates on this in Galatians 3:6-7, **"Even so Abraham believed God, and it was reckoned to him as righteousness. Therefore, be sure that it is those who are of faith who are sons of Abraham."** We are not the heirs of faith because we know that we must live by faith, but we become the heirs of faith by actually having faith, by doing the same deeds that Abraham did. We must devote ourselves to finding what the Lord is building and sacrifice whatever is required to be a part of it.

Abraham was apparently from a noble family in what was then the greatest culture on the earth. They had science and technology that surpassed any other culture of the time. The Chaldeans were the custodians of the great wonders of the world, but something burned in Abraham's heart to be a part of something much greater than anything men could build. He believed God by being willing to leave everything that he had known, the greatest life available at that time, to seek the Lord's will in unknown places. Faith sees far beyond what others can see. Faith sees with the eyes of the heart, and walks more by what is seen by the heart than what is seen by physical eyes.

Why is faith so important to God? Why doesn't He just reveal Himself and make it clear what He expects of us? Because He is seeking sons and daughters who will be joint heirs with His Son. It was doubting God that brought about the fall of man, and it will be by believing Him that we are restored. True faith rises from the heart, not just the head.

Satan dwelt in the very throne room of God, saw all of His glory, and still fell. Just seeing the Lord will not keep us from falling. As His joint heirs, He is going to trust us with more power than Satan ever had. We are now proving by our faith and obedience that we love the truth, and we love Him, more than we love even our own lives.

Even though we can fall even when beholding the glory of the Lord, as Satan proved, it is hard not to worship the Lord while we are beholding His glory. For all of eternity the whole creation will know that His sons and daughters worshiped Him, and stood for His truth, against the opposition of the whole world that now lies in the power of the evil one. After the fall, Satan could boast that even in a perfect world, man chose to rebel against God. By this he has justified his own rebellion. Now even his own principalities and powers have beheld the witness of those who lived in a most imperfect world, and even when all hell raged against them, they loved the Lord and obeyed Him at even the cost of their lives. These are the ones who all of creation will testify that they are worthy.

Therefore, walk in a manner worthy of your calling. Believe God. Obey Him. Do all things for the sake of His gospel, and let the love of Christ control you. He is worthy of our obedience and faith.

> **To this end also we pray for you always that our God may count you worthy of your calling, and fulfill every desire for goodness and the work of faith with power;**
>
> **in order that the name of our Lord Jesus may be glorified in you, and you in Him, according to the grace of our God and the Lord Jesus Christ (II Thessalonians 1:11-12).**

> **For I consider that the sufferings of this present time are not worthy to be compared with the glory that is to be revealed to us.**
>
> **For the anxious longing of the creation waits eagerly for the revealing of the sons of God.**
>
> **For the creation was subjected to futility, not of its own will, but because of Him who subjected it, in hope**
>
> **that the creation itself also will be set free from its slavery to corruption into the freedom of the glory of the children of God.**

For we know that the whole creation groans and suffers the pains of childbirth together until now.

And not only this, but also we ourselves, having the first fruits of the Spirit, even we ourselves groan within ourselves, waiting eagerly for our adoption as sons, the redemption of our body.

For in hope we have been saved, but hope that is seen is not hope; for why does one also hope for what he sees?

But if we hope for what we do not see, with perseverance we wait eagerly for it (Romans 8:18-25).